The Return of Jesus Christ

An introduction to the events
leading up to, and covering,
the return of the Lord Jesus Christ,
His Millennial reign on earth,
and Eternity —
as prophesied in the Holy Bible

By

Richard F Salmon

Cover design by R F Salmon

© Copyright 2005 Richard F. Salmon

Note for Librarians: A cataloguing record for this book is available from Library and Archives
Canada at www.collectionscanada.ca/amicus/index-e.html
ISBN 1-4120-5484-2

*Printed in Victoria, BC, Canada. Printed on paper with minimum 30% recycled fibre. Trafford's print shop runs
on "green energy" from solar, wind and other environmentally-friendly power sources.*

TRAFFORD
PUBLISHING™

Offices in Canada, USA, Ireland and UK

Book sales for North America and international:
Trafford Publishing, 6E–2333 Government St.,
Victoria, BC V8T 4P4 CANADA
phone 250 383 6864 (toll-free 1 888 232 4444)
fax 250 383 6804; email to orders@trafford.com
Book sales in Europe:
Trafford Publishing (UK) Limited, 9 Park End Street, 2nd Floor
Oxford, UK OX1 1HH UNITED KINGDOM
phone 44 (0)1865 722 113 (local rate 0845 230 9601)
facsimile 44 (0)1865 722 868; info.uk@trafford.com
Order online at:
trafford.com/05-0382

10 9 8 7 6

To a nameless elderly Canadian Christian gentleman,
and Paul Veitch, Brian Fruish & Ken Rout,
whom God used to bring me to Christ.

Contents

Forward

While I was a deck hand in my teens on a Merchant ship docked in St. John, Newfoundland, an elderly Christian man came aboard and gave me a New Testament. It was like handing me a time bomb! Though I had had a background of Sunday School and church upbringing, the New Testament that he gave me was what the Spirit of God used to convict me that I was not right with God and that hell awaited the pleasure of my company.

Two years later, on a street in Wellington New Zealand, on the night of Sunday 3rd October 1971, a man named Paul Veitch stopped and talked to me about Jesus Christ and His salvation. Two 'Open Air Campaigners', Brian Fruish and Ken Rout, took over from Paul and led me to the foot of Jesus' cross that night. There, praise God, I found forgiveness of my sins and eternal life, through the precious shed blood, death and resurrection of Jesus Christ.

Since the night I came to know Jesus Christ as my Saviour, my Christian walk has had its mountain peaks and deep valleys. Over the years since my conversion, sin and failure, like mad raving dogs snarling at my feet, have bitten deep into my life more than once. It was through such times that I found God's love immeasurable and His forgiveness unfathomable. I wondered how such a holy and righteous God could want anything more to do with me since I had let Him down so badly in my Christian testimony. But through it all, the Lord has taught me more of His great love and the necessity of coming back to the cross every day to seek His forgiveness and cleansing. He is always there to forgive, heal and restore His wounded child. I have also realised the need to feed on God's word, and to pray to Him daily, for the spiritual strength to get me through each day. To neglect talking with Him and reading His word is more foolish than to remain silent in the company of good friends and refusing to eat good food they have put before me.

What has kept me going over these years is the thought that the Lord Jesus could come back at any moment, and, according to His own word, I have simply wanted to be ready when He comes (Matthew 24:44).

I have been very keen on the study of prophecy since the beginning of my Christian life and I have read many books on the subject. But at the end of the day it is so necessary to come back to the word of God to see exactly what *He* says. This short book, which includes lots of quotations and references from scripture, is intended for those Christians, and others, who want a simple, short and hopefully easy-to-understand explanation of what God has planned for this world, for Christians and non Christians. It should be read only as an introduction to the subject.

I want to thank my friends and fellow Christians, Mr. Howard Hawes and Mrs. Zoe Burden, for reading over my work and making corrections to spelling and grammar, and for making helpful suggestions.

Titles of other books and their authors, which deal with the subject more fully than I do and may be helpful, are given in the bibliography. I trust this one will be a blessing to all who take the time to read it.

Richard F. Salmon.

Introduction

When I was a boy at school in the 1950s and 60s I remember how that the twenty-first century seemed to be about as far away as the edge of the universe. Yet here we are! The amazing speed at which technology advanced in the twentieth century has had us all gasping in wonder and amazement. Yet, for all the technological progress those one hundred years produced, it also witnessed the two most devastating wars, in the history of man, in which around 55 million people lost their lives. Wars and genocide, corruption and violence go on to this day and still nobody seems to be able to put a stop to them.

Apart from killing each other, man has spent, and continues to spend, billions of pounds on space technology with a view to manned space exploration. Meanwhile, back on earth, hundreds of thousands of innocent and helpless people continue to die every year for want of a loaf of bread and a drink of water. All of which goes to prove that morally, man has not learned a thing. So why doesn't God do something about it? Why (when the Lord Jesus was sent by His Father 2000 years ago to be the Saviour of the world), does the world continue on in its way, and why do things seem to be getting worse rather than better? Why is God waiting? For what are we waiting?

God is gracious and merciful and He tells us in His word that He is " ... *patient with* [us], *not wanting anyone to perish, but everyone to come to repentance*" (2 Peter 3:9), and to this end:

" *... these* [things about Jesus] *are written that* [we] *may believe that Jesus is the Christ, the Son of God, and that by believing* [we] *may have life in His name."*

John 20:31

So what does God mean by "repentance" and "believing" in Jesus Christ the Son of God? What exactly are these things that He is looking for in us?

Well, repentance means to "turn around" or to "change" in our outlook and attitude towards 1) God, 2) others and 3) our sinful selves.

1) Our attitude towards God. If we have ignored or have simply tended to disregard God and His word, it's time to sit up and take notice of Him and to listen to what He says in the Bible about Himself, Jesus Christ, our sinful condition and His judgment that, one day, will surely come.

2) Our attitude towards others. Have we been unhelpful, nasty or even aggressive to other people? Have we tricked, deceived or stolen from other people who were doing nothing to harm or wrong us in any way? Then it's time to stop that sort of behaviour and to start treating people and their property with respect.

3) Our attitude towards our sinful selves. Do we have our own idea about God that says we can go through life doing what we like and then expect Him to receive us into heaven when we die? Do we think that God will just turn a blind eye to all the wrong that we have done in our lives, and receive us into heaven at last, because we think we don't deserve anything less? Then it's about time we stopped deceiving ourselves and seek to find out exactly what the truth is about ourselves and our relationship with our Creator God.

Some might say, "I don't believe in the existence of God." But God tells us that He has made known His glorious and powerful existence to everyone, including you:

"The heavens declare the glory of God; the skies proclaim the work of His hands. Day after day they pour forth speech; night after night they display knowledge. There is no speech or language where their voice is not heard. Their voice goes out into all the earth, their words to the ends of the world. ..."

Psalm 19:1-4

"The wrath of God is being revealed from heaven against all the godlessness and wickedness of men who suppress the truth by their wickedness, since what may be known about God is plain to them, **because God has made it plain to them***. For since the creation of the world God's invisible qualities - His eternal power and divine nature - have been clearly seen, being understood from what has been made,* **so that men are without excuse***. For although they knew God, they neither glorified Him as God nor gave thanks to Him, but their thinking became futile and their foolish hearts were darkened. Although they claimed to be wise, they became fools and exchanged the glory of the immortal God for images made to look like mortal man and birds and animals and reptiles. Therefore God gave them over in the sinful desires of their hearts to sexual impurity for the degrading of their bodies with one another.* **They exchanged the truth of God for a lie***, and worshipped and served created things rather than the Creator - who is forever praised. Amen."* (Emphasis added)

Romans 1:18-25

You see, God has spoken to you of His existence and eternal power and glory through His creation and by witnessing to you in your heart. If you now refuse to believe in the existence of God it is because you have made a deliberate choice not to believe in Him, even though, at some time in your life, you did.

So what about "believing"? When God talks about believing in His Son Jesus Christ He is not meaning a casual, "I've heard about him" type of believing. We might believe that Mount Everest exists, but only on the testimony and photographs of others. Most of us have never been there, so we have never experienced what it is like to stand on that huge mountain. If we wanted a first hand understanding of it, we would have to go there and face it for ourselves. This is what God means to "believe" in Jesus. Others might tell us about Jesus and what He has done to save us from our sins, but we need to go to Him and experience Him for ourselves. We cannot be saved on the hearsay and experience of others. We need to approach God, in our hearts, for ourselves - to rely on and trust in Him with all our heart. This is what we call faith. Faith is to take God at His word. God says it, so we must believe it.

> "... faith is the substance of things hoped for, the evidence of things not seen."
>
> Hebrews 11:1 (AV)

We will only fully understand the necessity of our putting our faith and trust in Jesus when we come to realise that our sinful state, and our sins, have separated us from God and we deserve His judgment. Jesus Christ came into this world to be our Saviour by taking God's judgment against our sins for us by dying on the cross. There, in His great love for a world of lost and sinful people, He paid the price necessary for us to be forgiven for our sins and to receive eternal life from God. The Apostle John tells us this good news message in this way:

> *"For God so loved the world that he gave His only begotten Son, that whoever believes in Him shall not perish but have eternal life. For God did not send His Son into the world to condemn the world, but to save the world through Him. Whoever believes in Him is not condemned, but whoever does not believe stands condemned already because he has not believed in the name of God's only begotten Son."*
>
> John 3:16-18

And the Apostle Paul puts our sinful condition and what Jesus has done for us like this:

> *"For the wages of sin is death, but the gift of God is eternal life through Christ Jesus our Lord."*
>
> Romans 6:23

So while it appears that the world carries on with a God in heaven who seems to be doing nothing about the sinful and depraved state of mankind, the wars, disasters, famines and atrocities that are happening in many countries, this is in fact only a delusion on the part of man. God will one day step in and take over from man in running this world. He has warned us that:

> *"... He has set a day when He will judge the world with justice*

by the Man [Jesus] *He has appointed. He has given proof of this to all men by raising him from the dead.*"

Acts 17:3

If God has appointed a day to judge the world, then it can only be getting closer and closer, morning by morning. To ignore this is nothing less than perilous.

Those who have put their faith and trust in Jesus Christ for the forgiveness of their sins know that there is nothing to fear. On the contrary, it is with great excitement and anticipation that true Christian believers are waiting for the return of the Lord Jesus Christ. For He has surely promised that He will come back and take them to be with Himself.

> "*Do not let your hearts be troubled. Trust in God, trust also in Me. In My Fathers house are many rooms; if it were not so, I would have told you. I am going there to prepare a place for you. And if I go and prepare a place for you,* **I will come back and take you to be with Me** *that you also may be where I am.*" (Emphasis added)

John 14:1-3

These are comforting words for those who know Jesus Christ as their Saviour and Lord. Those Christians who have died, their souls have gone to be with the Lord in Heaven and, when Jesus comes back, they will be resurrected from the dead and given new immortal, sinless and glorious bodies. Those who are still alive when Jesus comes again will be changed in the same way. Both the resurrected Christians, and those who have been changed, will be caught up into Heaven together, to be with the Lord forever (1 Thessalonians 4:13-18).

There have been many books written about the prophecies in the Bible concerning the return of the Lord Jesus Christ and the things that are going to happen in the world at that time. Many writers have written sensible and helpful books. Others have jumped into sensational speculation while yet still others have foolishly set dates, totally ignoring what Jesus said just before He went back into Heaven.

> *"Therefore keep watch, because **you do not know** on what day your Lord will come."* (Emphasis added)
>
> Matthew 24:42

Not only do we not know when the Day of The Lord will come, but it is in God's purposes to withhold that information from us.

> *"He said to them: '**It is not for you to know** the times or dates the Father has set by His own authority.'"* (Emphasis added)
>
> Acts 1:7

There is a great increase in false (so-called Christian) prophets these days who are increasing in popularity among many professing Christians and of whom they should beware. They voice their apparent revelations, which they are supposedly having from God, and are confusing many innocent Christians who are genuinely seeking to know God's determined plan for the last days. Everything spoken or written in regards to God's truth should be tested against Scripture. God does not contradict himself either by word or by principle.

Unfortunately, some have been so carried away that they

have suggested certain religious, political, national or world figures to be the Antichrist. In their opinion, the Antichrist has supposed to have been Napoleon, Hitler, Mussolini and various Popes to name a few! All of which claims have proved very wrong.

As the year 2000 approached, some people were afraid that some cataclysmic event might engulf the earth as we passed midnight on 31 December 1999. But it came and went as any other new year. So, after all the 'hype' and then the anticlimax of entering a new millennium, the world has settled down again to its everyday routines.

The following expanded work began life as a series of short monthly papers written as an introduction to the subject of the return of Jesus Christ. They were developed for interested Christians throughout 1999 when I was a member of Castlehold Baptist Church in Newport on the Isle of Wight. The idea then, as now, has been to keep things simple and to the point.

It is hoped that the reader of this short book will be encouraged to read for themselves what the Lord has to say in His own Word, the Holy Bible, about the return of Jesus Christ and associated events, rather than reading only this or any other books on prophecy. There are many prophecies scattered throughout the scriptures concerning the Second Advent of Christ and, with careful study, it will be seen that they all fit together like a jigsaw. Do not be put off if, at first, things seem too difficult to understand! Be patient, and think on the scriptures you have read, and prayerfully ask the Lord to show you what He is saying in these prophecies. After all, if He didn't want you to know, He wouldn't have put them there in the first place!

The following should be looked upon as no more than an introduction to the study of the Lord's return. It goes out with the desire and prayer that those who read its pages will be both helped and blessed from doing so. The work is written with the hope that it is in keeping with the words of the Lord Jesus when He said:

> *"Blessed is the one who reads the words of this prophecy, and ... those who ... take to heart what is written in it, because the time is near."*

Revelation 1:3

AN OVERALL PICTURE

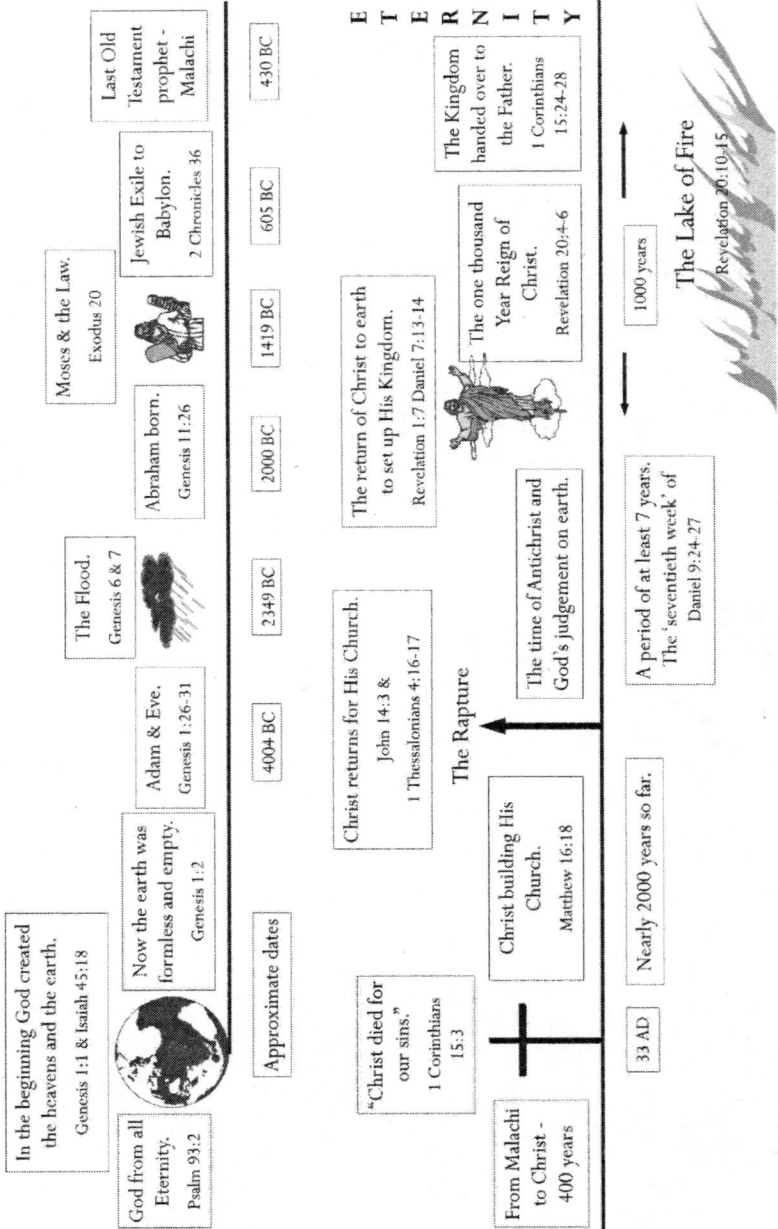

In the beginning God created the heavens and the earth. Genesis 1:1 & Isaiah 45:18

Now the earth was formless and empty. Genesis 1:2

God from all Eternity. Psalm 93:2

The Flood. Genesis 6 & 7

Adam & Eve. Genesis 1:26-31

Moses & the Law. Exodus 20

Abraham born. Genesis 11:26

Jewish Exile to Babylon. 2 Chronicles 36

Last Old Testament prophet - Malachi

Approximate dates

4004 BC 2349 BC 2000 BC 1419 BC 605 BC 430 BC

"Christ died for our sins." 1 Corinthians 15:3

Christ building His Church. Matthew 16:18

Christ returns for His Church. John 14:3 & 1 Thessalonians 4:16-17

The Rapture

The time of Antichrist and God's judgement on earth.

A period of at least 7 years. The 'seventieth week' of Daniel 9:24-27

The return of Christ to earth to set up His Kingdom. Revelation 1:7 Daniel 7:13-14

The one thousand Year Reign of Christ. Revelation 20:4-6

The Kingdom handed over to the Father. 1 Corinthians 15:24-28

ETERNITY

1000 years

The Lake of Fire. Revelation 20:10,15

33 AD

From Malachi to Christ - 400 years

Nearly 2000 years so far.

1

An Overall Picture

To begin with, it might be a good idea to view an overall plan of God's dealings with man as far as we can ascertain them from the scriptures. Firstly, there was Creation. Here it must be understood that times and dates, though approximate, are given in relation to the years as revealed in the Holy Scriptures and not the ideas of Evolution, an as yet unproven theory, or to any other preconceived ideas of the age of the world or to how long man has inhabited the earth. So when God created the earth (as recorded in Genesis chapters 1 and 2) and made man from the dust of the earth and placed him in the Garden of Eden, it has been calculated to be approximately 4000 years BC. The flood of Noah's day would be approximately 2349 BC; Abraham 2000 BC; Moses and God's Law given 1419 BC; the Israelites captive in Babylon 605 BC; and the last Old Testament prophet, Malachi, appeared 430 years before Christ was born in Bethlehem. These dates are those generally accepted as being as accurate as can be deduced, and are based on the calculations of Archbishop James Ussher. Not every major event has been included here, but I hope that the events which are included will help the reader to grasp something of the time scale from Adam and Eve to Christ which covers something like 4000 years. From the birth of our Lord Jesus Christ till now is roughly 2000 years, so from Adam and Eve's day till now is approximately 6000 years. [1]

An idea held by some is the 'Septa-Millennial Theory,'

the emphasis being on 'theory' so as not to mistake it for Biblical revelation. The Septa-Millennial Theory has come about through the idea that each day of creation represents 1000 years. So six days of creation equals 6000 years, plus the seventh day when God rested from all His work, which is another 1000 years, making a period of 7000 years in all.

The Lord Jesus is to reign as King on earth for 1000 years:

> *"Blessed and holy are those who have part in the first resurrection. The second death has no power over them, but they will be priests of God and of Christ and will reign with Him for a thousand years."*
>
> Revelation 20:6

This is to be a time of rest for the people of God:

> *"There remains, then, a Sabbath-rest for the people of God."*
>
> Hebrews 4:9

So it is reasoned that if God worked six days in creation and rested on the seventh, the Sabbath, there will be 6000 years when man is responsible to govern on earth, and God works through men, and then a 1000 year period of Sabbath rest when Jesus reigns over all nations as King of kings and Lord of lords. Along with this is Peter's declaration that:

> *"With the Lord a day is like a thousand years, and a thousand years are like a day."*
>
> 2 Peter 3:8

The table below may be helpful for understanding this idea.

Days of Creation	Years of The World
Day 1.........	........1000 years
Day 2.........	........2000 years
Day 3.........	........3000 years
Day 4.........	........4000 years
Day 5.........	........5000 years
Day 6.........	........6000 years
Day 7.........	........7000 years

Apparently this theory is not new. It is supposed to have its origins among the Jews, BC, and was based solely on the assumption that the Messiah would reign for 1000 years. It just so happens that the 6000 year period is drawing to a close, so if the theory is correct, it means that the Lord's 1000 year reign will soon be upon us. Time alone will tell!

What must be emphasised is that nowhere does scripture tell us when the Lord Jesus will come back for His Church. Jesus Himself was very clear about that:

*"Therefore keep watch, because **you do not know** on what day your Lord will come."* (Emphasis added)

Matthew 24:42

The Apostle Paul also said the same thing:

"Now, brothers, about times and dates we do not need to write to you, for you know very well that the day of the Lord will come like a thief in the night."

Thessalonians 5:1-2

From these words we can deduce that the Lord's return for His Church will be sudden and without warning. However, Christians should be expecting Him and eager for His return at all times!

> *"But our citizenship is in heaven. And we eagerly await a Saviour from there, the Lord Jesus Christ."*
> Philippians 3:20

Footnotes:

[1] I know that, because the theory of Evolution has been taught, virtually as fact, in schools and the media for so long now, many will scorn the idea that man has only been around for approximately 6000 years. But if we are to approach God and His word to understand His creation and His dealings with mankind and the world, we have to realise that God is a God of truth; He does not lie and He does not deceive. That is the great adversary's work. Satan (oh yes, he really does exist) is the liar and deceiver of mankind and from the very beginning, when Adam and Eve were in the Garden of Eden, he has sought to turn man away from God's truth. With the technological advances in science and astronomy over the last few years, the theory of evolution, if anything, is actually being proved to be completely impossible. Creation and the universe are, apparently, so mathematically precise, that only a Creator God could make something so intricately detailed and finely balanced. It now appears that to consider that the very simplest forms of life could just happen by chance is simply impossible, and to think that such basic life forms that are found on earth could 'evolve' into a more intricate and intelligent life form is about as likely as a rock fall from a mountainside ending up in the valley below as a three story eight bed roomed home!

AN OVERVIEW OF THE CHURCH AGE

The Seven Churches. Revelation chapters 1, 2 & 3.

	Ephesus Meaning - (Desirable)	Smyrna Meaning - (Myrrh or bitterness)	Pergamos Meaning - (Married)	Thyatira Meaning - (Sacrifice)	Sardis Meaning - (Remnant)	Philadelphia Meaning - (Brotherly love)	Laodicea Meaning - (The people rule)	
	Hard work & perseverance - but forsaken first love	Afflicted and poor - but rich	True to His Name - but hold wrong teaching	Love, faith, service & perseverance - but immorality	Reputation of being alive - but dead	A little strength, Have kept My Word, not denied My name	Lukewarm, wretched pitiful, poor, blind & naked	
AD 33	AD 33-150	AD 150-300	AD 300-600	AD 600-1500	AD 1500-1750	AD 1750-1900	AD 1900-present	Any moment
The Holy Spirit given and the Church born	The Apostolic Church. Young and energetic, but loosing its first love for Jesus	The Church suffers persecution from Rome	The Church united to the state, and thus to the world	The dark ages, The Church suppresses the truth, Papacy rules and sexual immorality is tolerated	The lifeless Church from which a remnant come & return to the word of God	The evangelical Church with missionary outlook and which keeps to God's word	The sickening Church of self proclaimed wealth and self importance	The Church taken to heaven

Holy Spirit

Pentecost

The Rapture

In every church, without exception, the promise of reward is given to those who overcome

2

An Overview of the Church Age

By 'the Church Age' in this chapter title, we are referring to the time during which Christ is building His church (Matthew 16:18), that is, from Pentecost when it began and when the Holy Spirit was given, until the Lord Jesus returns for the Church, *"which is His body"* (Ephesians 1:23). The Church is made up of every single person who has ever trusted in Christ alone for the forgiveness of their sins, from every nation and walk of life, old and young, rich or poor.

The apostle Paul referred to this present time in which Christ is building His Church as *'the fulfilment of the ages'* (1 Corinthians 10:11). The writer to the Hebrews refers to it as *'these last days'* (Hebrews 1:2) and Peter as *'these last times'* (1 Peter 1:20). God is bringing to conclusion in our day all that has gone before:

> *"And He made known to us the mystery of His will, according to His good pleasure, which He purposed in Christ, to be put into effect when the times have reached their fulfilment - to bring all things in heaven and on earth together under one head, even Christ."*
>
> Ephesians 1:9-10

To say that the times in which we live are exciting is an understatement; they're mind blowing! The conclusion to this age in which we live is that Jesus Christ will return and remove all evil and all that offends God from the world. There will be no more wars, famines or natural catastrophes, as there have been down through history. There will no longer be the rise, or the threat, of wicked dictators who oppress their people and keep them in bondage to their evil political systems. Instead:

"The Lord will be King over the whole earth."

Zechariah 14:9

This King, none other than the Lord Jesus Christ Himself, will reign in righteousness and justice (Psalm 9:8 & Isaiah 32:1) and no one will need fear any oppressor.

At the end of the Bible, we read of seven churches in Asia and the words John was told by the Lord Jesus to write down and send them. They are found in the book of Revelation chapters 1 to 3. What is said to these seven local churches could perhaps be applied to the situation of some Christians in any area in the world in our day besides the obvious and immediate context. For instance, we could apply the situation of the church at Smyrna to Christians in several countries in the world today, for some believers suffer terrible persecution, even to death, from the authorities and/or their fellow citizens because they dare to stand up and witness to their Saviour Jesus Christ.

The things said to these seven churches in Asia could also be applicable to any local church in any area of the world today, or any century for that matter, for the spiritual condition of believers does differ from one local church to another. Also, having the benefit of hindsight, we can follow the general spiritual state of believers in the world from Pentecost, AD 33, when the Church was born, up to the present day. The seven local churches specifically mentioned, with their particular trials, needs and failings, appear to be indicative of the different spiritual conditions through which Christians, in the world, would pass down through the ages.

Ephesus (meaning desirable) AD 33-150, the early Apostolic Church, young and energetic but losing its first love for Jesus; Smyrna (meaning myrrh or bitterness) AD 150-300, the Church suffers persecution from Rome; Pergamos (meaning married) AD 300-600, the Church is united to the State, and thus to the world, by Constantine; Thyatira (meaning sacrifice) AD 600-1500, the dark ages where the Church suppresses the truth, Papacy rules and sexual immorality is tolerated; Sardis (meaning remnant) AD 1500-1750, the lifeless Church from which a remnant come and return to the truth of the Word of God; Philadelphia (meaning brotherly love) AD 1750-1900, the evangelical Church with missionary outlook which keeps to God's Word; Laodicea (meaning the people rule) AD 1900-last days, the sickening Church of self proclaimed wealth and self importance.

Most students of prophecy agree with the dates given for each successive period, give or take a few years.

The fact that a double meaning may be applied to each of the seven statements in no way detracts from the importance of the immediate context of these letters, of course. They were real local churches to which the Lord Jesus was speaking. We would not want to be a part of a local church today where the Lord stands outside knocking to come in, as at Laodicea. The local church there seemed to have a lot going for it. They were rich, had acquired wealth and needed nothing. That's not a sin in itself. The problem was, that like the church at Ephesus, they had their eyes so fixed on 'things THEY had' and 'things THEY were doing' that they had lost sight of the One who died for them.

The commission of the Lord Jesus to His followers is:

"Therefore go and make disciples of all nations, baptising them in the Name of the Father, and of the Son and of the Holy Spirit, and teaching them to obey everything I have commanded you. And surely I am with you always, to the very end of the age."

Matthew 28:19-20

But His commission does not go without warning to His disciples:

"If the world hates you, keep in mind that it hated Me first. If you belonged to the world, it would love you as its own. As it is, you do not belong to the world, but I have chosen you out of the world. That is why the world hates you. Remember the words I spoke to you: 'No servant is greater than his master.' If they persecuted Me, they will persecute you also."

John 15:18-20

"They will do such things because they have not known the Father or Me. I have told you this, so that when the time comes you will remember that I warned you."

John 16:3-4

"I have told you these things, so that in Me you may have peace. In this world you will have trouble. But take heart! I have overcome the world."

John 16:33

God wants Christians to be 'over comers' of this world and all that it stands for. To be in the world for sure, but not of it. For that reason the Lord Jesus promises to be with Christians always, to the very end of the age. Many Christians today, especially in the westernised countries, are living in a very Laodicean way of materialism and friendship with the world. It is no wonder that the Lord is seen standing at the door of the church at Laodicea knocking to come in. Many Christians today have so much religion and 'churchianity' that there is little room for Christ and the truth of the Gospel in their hearts and lives! But while they are still alive in the world there remains opportunity for them to be revived in their hearts by the Holy Spirit, if they are willing, and to turn back to the Lord. Many Christians call out and pray to God for revival, not realising that revival is had by their simply turning form their sinful ways, returning to God and His word in obedience and walking in His ways (1 John 1:9, 2:15-17). It is then, in willingness and obedience to do God's will, that we shall eat, in the spiritual sense, *"the best from the land"* (Isaiah 1:19).

There are no specific events prophesied in the New Testament for this present age before the return of Jesus Christ for His Church. Rather than being like the Pharisees and Sadducees who were rebuked by Jesus for not interpreting the signs of the times in their day (Matthew 16:1-4), we are expected to be aware of the 'signs' of His second coming:

> *"When these things begin to take place, stand up and lift up your heads, because your redemption is drawing near ... Be always on the watch."*
>
> Luke 21:28 & 36

SIGNS OF HIS COMING IN THE CHURCHES

A 'Laodicean' type Church

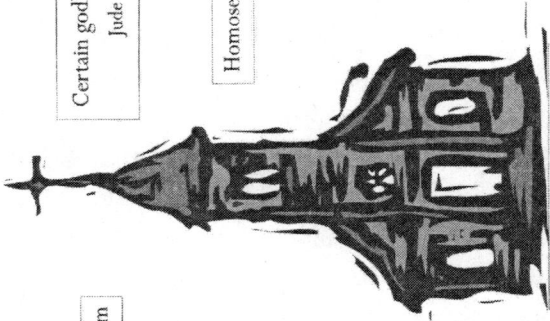

Men will not put up with sound doctrine. They will turn their ears away from the truth and turn aside to myths.

2 Timothy 4:3-4

Transcendental Meditation

Men of depraved minds will oppose the truth.

2 Timothy 3:8

Those who profess to be Christians and who apparently do miraculous things, but who have never truly known the Lord as their Saviour.

Matthew 7:21-23

Certain godless men.

Jude 4

Homosexuality

Jesus stands at the door and knocks to come in.

Revelation 3:20

New Ageism

Men who distort God's truth in order to draw away disciples after them.

Acts 20:30

The Spirit clearly says that in the later times some will abandon the faith and follow deceiving spirits and things taught by demons.

1 Timothy 4:1

False teachers, secretly intro-ducing destructive heresies. Many will follow their shameful ways.

2 Peter 2:1

Lukewarmness.

Revelation 3:16

Laodicea means 'The people rule' or 'Will of the people'

3

Signs of His Coming in the Churches

It should be pointed out that the title of this chapter is referring to local churches of believers that gather together unto the Lord's Name (Matthew 18:20), and not any particular mainstream denomination that most people associate with "The Church". [1]

There are two areas in which we see signs that lead us to believe that we are in the last days. Firstly, there are signs in the churches; those things which we are told will occur and which include the general spiritual condition of many, to which we have referred in the previous chapter. It bears repeating that we are not told at what point the Lord will return for His Church *which is His body*" (Ephesians 1:22-23), but that we should "expect" Him at any time.

Secondly, there are the signs in the world. These relate particularly to our Lord's return to earth, and lead on to certain specific events that are prophesied in Scripture. These will be plain for all the world to see and will be dealt with in the next chapter.

The indication given to us in the New Testament regarding the churches is that they will deteriorate morally and spiritually into quite a 'mixed bag'. The Lord tells us several parables to this effect. One notable passage is to be found in Matthew chapter 13:24-43, 47-52, where the Lord speaks about 'the kingdom of heaven'. In the context of what the Lord says in that passage, He seems to imply that the kingdom of heaven on earth, made up of true believers, would also be a dwelling place for those who profess to be Christians, but who have never been truly "born again". What we might refer to as 'Christendom'.

In the first parable referred to, the 'kingdom of heaven' is likened to a field (verse 24). True believers are represented by the good seed, or wheat, among which the enemy sows weeds (sons of the evil one). *"Let both grow together until the harvest"*, the servants are told (verse 30). Then the weeds will be bundled up to be burned and the wheat gathered into the barn. A picture, if you will, of on the one hand those unsaved who are cast into hell and, on the other hand, those taken to be with the Lord in heaven.

Again, 'the kingdom of heaven' is like a small mustard seed which, when fully grown, is large enough to shelter all sorts of birds (suggesting that those who do not belong to God's kingdom shelter amongst those that do). And again, it is like dough in which yeast has been placed until it permeates the whole. In Scripture, yeast almost always speaks of sin.

We are told that the 'kingdom of heaven' is like a net, which, when it is full of fish, is pulled up to shore where the good fish are collected into baskets and the bad fish are thrown away. From these statements we can only conclude that there will be a lot of people who profess to be Christians but who really are not. They are weeds, birds or bad fish! They may, outwardly, appear to be believers, but they have never been truly born again.

It may seem almost inconceivable that some people could actually go to a church week after week, maybe all their lives in fact, and hear the word of God being preached - even taking part in some way, perhaps even in leadership - and yet not be a true Christian. But there is plenty of evidence in the scriptures that such a situation could, and does, exist.

When the Lord was speaking in Matthew 7:21-23 He said that not every one who says to Him, "Lord", would enter the kingdom of heaven. He said that "many" would speak about what they had done in His Name, but He refers to them as "evildoers"! In Luke's account, Jesus tells us that these false Christians would also plead with Him to open the door for them because they had eaten and drunk in His presence (perhaps a reference to their participation in the Lord's Supper) and that He had taught in their streets. But again, He refers to them as evildoers. It is little wonder then that we are told:

> *"Examine yourselves to see whether you are in the faith; test yourselves. Do you not realize that Christ Jesus is in you - unless, of course, you fail the test?"*
>
> 2 Corinthians 13:5

And what is our test? Well, we should make sure that we are trusting in Jesus Christ alone for the forgiveness of sins and not anything else.

It may be as well to comment here on two particular 'mindsets' which have become, or are becoming, popular among many churches:

Firstly, for quite a number of years there has been a growing number of believers who, having professed faith in Christ, have been persuaded that there is some other experience that they need. This has been called by various names but is most commonly known as the 'Baptism of the Spirit.' Recently this has been broadened and has developed into what is known as the 'Toronto Blessing'. This experience is accompanied by speaking in other unfamiliar languages (tongues) and/or, falling to the floor in somewhat uncontrollable states of laughter, or making noises similar to those of animals!

You might be surprised to know that there are some churches that actually promote this kind of so called 'worship'! It is quite likely that there may be one near you, whether it is one of the larger mainstream denominations or a smaller, more openly charismatic group.

If these phenomena were from God, and vitally important aspects of the believer's walk with Him, we would expect to find them taught regularly, as such, in scripture, which we patently do not. Speaking in 'tongues' is recorded only three times in the book of Acts and occurs only when the Lord is initiating some new momentous event:

First, at Jerusalem, when the Holy Spirit was first given to Jewish believers:

> *"All of them were filled with the Holy Spirit and began to speak in other tongues* [languages] *as the Spirit enabled them."*
>
> Acts 2:4

Second, at the house of Cornelius, when the Holy Spirit was first poured out on Gentile believers:

> *"The circumcised believers* [Jews] *... were astonished that the gift of the Holy Spirit had been poured out even on the Gentiles for they heard them speaking in tongues* [other languages] *and praising God."*
>
> Acts 10: 45-46

Third, at Ephesus, when about twelve disciples who knew only the teaching of John the Baptist came to believe in Jesus. On being told about Him by Paul, they were baptised straight away in the name of the Lord Jesus:

> *"When Paul placed his hands on them, the Holy Spirit came on them, and they spoke in tongues* [other languages] *and prophesied."*
>
> Acts 19:6

We read twice in the book of Acts how believers would be baptised with the Holy Spirit: firstly in chapter 1:5 and secondly Peter's remembrance of that day in chapter 11:16. Let's read exactly what was being referred to by this event.

> *"When the day of Pentecost came, they were all together in one place. Suddenly a sound like the blowing of a violent wind came from heaven and filled the whole house where they were sitting. They saw what seemed to be tongues of fire that separated and came to rest on each of them. All of them were filled with the Holy Spirit and began to speak in other tongues* [languages] *as the Spirit enabled them."*
>
> Acts 2:1-4

Here, we have the giving of the Holy Spirit in a very special way, as referred to in chapter 1:5. The word "baptise" is a word borrowed straight out of the Greek language, in which the early scriptures were written, and is spelt *BAPTIZO*. It comes from a shorter word *BAPTO* which means simply 'to dip' or 'to immerse' something. The thought behind this means to immerse a garment in a liquid dye so as to stain it (a thought brought out in Revelation 19:13 where we read of Jesus' robe *"dipped [BAPTO] in blood."*) To be baptised or *BAPTIZO* then, is the act of being *BAPTO*, dipped or immersed, and is usually associated with water baptism after conversion.

With this understanding of the word 'baptise', we can understand what actually happened to the believers on the day of Pentecost. They were immersed in the Holy Spirit, something that God had never before done to believers.

The 'Baptism of the Spirit' is mentioned only once after the book of Acts, in 1 Corinthians:

> *"For **we were all baptised by one Spirit into one body** - whether Jews or Greeks, slave or free - and **we were all given the one Spirit to drink**."* (Emphasis added)
>
> 1 Corinthians 12:13

Notice in that verse the three words, *"we were all"*! Not 'some of us were' or 'most of us were' neither 'we must be' or 'we should be'. *"We were all"* is all inclusive of all believers!

Peter preached,

> *"Repent and be baptised* [in water], *every one of you, in the name of Jesus Christ for the forgiveness of your sins. And **you will receive the gift of the Holy Spirit**."* (Emphasis added)
>
> Acts 2:38

This would indicate that everyone who trusts in the Lord Jesus for salvation receives the gift of the Holy Spirit and is therefore baptised in Him at conversion. We do not need to look for nor to ask God for the baptism of the Holy Spirit at any time after our conversion experience, for He is already with us and we have been immersed in him.

> *"He* [God] *anointed us, set His seal of ownership on us, and* **put His Spirit in our hearts** *as a deposit, guaranteeing what is to come."* (Emphasis added)
>
> 2 Corinthians 1:21-22

Secondly, there is another evil creeping in among churches which, in part at least, is being embraced by many who don't know any better. It is ideas and teachings that come from what is commonly known as the New Age Movement.

Basically, New Age is a mixture of different spiritual, social and political elements, with the idea of changing people and society through spiritual awareness. It is often seen as resurgent paganism, and the modern movement has recent roots in 19th century spiritualism and in the 1960s anti-establishment mentality. It is keen to embrace Eastern mysticism and 'direct spiritual experience' rather than organised religion. The idea is to seek for self improvement and teaches that each individual has untapped capabilities including inner transformation and self healing. It is influenced by holistic thinking with regard to medicine, the family, the environment etc., and embraces a multiplicity of metaphysical and other ideas including reincarnation, aliens from outer space, the occult, shamanism, channelling, psychic healing, visualisation and yoga to name but a few! New Age is a real and active movement. It is subtle, it is evil and it is growing within many churches, especially among the young and unwary. God spoke through the apostle Paul and said:

> *"But I am afraid that just as Eve was deceived by the serpents cunning, your minds may somehow be led astray from your sincere and pure devotion to Christ. For if someone comes to you and preaches a Jesus other than the Jesus we preached, or if you receive a different spirit from the one you received, or a different gospel from the one you accepted, you put up with it easily enough."*
>
> 2 Corinthians 11:3-4

And again,

> *"Satan himself masquerades as an angel of light. It is not surprising, then, if his servants masquerade as servants of righteousness."*
>
> 2 Corinthians 11:14-15

It is not suggested that those who have become mixed up in these things have never been born again, though that might be the case in many instances, but we should never forget that the Devil is always busy trying to infiltrate the Christian ranks, seeking to turn the unsuspecting away from the truth by preaching a different Jesus and offering a different spirit because he wants people to believe a different gospel. The reason that the Devil is able to sow so many weeds among the wheat in these days is perhaps because the word of God has become tiresome to many. Like the Israelites of old, to whom God gave bread from heaven, many Christians are saying about the word of God:

> *"... We detest this miserable food!"*
>
> Numbers 21:5

Yet Christians are exhorted by Peter to:

"Desire the sincere milk of the word, that we may grow thereby."
1 Peter 2:2. (AV)

God tells Christians that they have been given *"fullness in Christ"* (Colossians 2:10); i.e., in Christ (in Whom *"the fullness of the Deity lives"* Colossians 2:9), Christians have all they need for forgiveness, salvation and eternal life, and for their needs in this life, until they are called by God into His eternal glorious presence in Heaven. So the suggestion that they need something else besides is quite wrong. Behind this thinking is the devilish deception that Christians are somehow incomplete in Christ: God has not given them all that they need, spiritually, in Christ. They should, so this satanic thinking suggests, do something about getting it. If that idea sounds familiar to you, it should, for it is the same lie of which the Devil convinced Eve in the Garden of Eden:

"…your eyes will be opened, and you will be like God."
Genesis 3:4

If Satan cannot beat Christians, he will join them, and is more than happy to pose as an 'angel of light' to get them to turn from the truth. The day is coming when he will be able openly to persecute Christians to death in westernised countries as he is currently doing in many other parts of the world today. In the meantime, here and now, he is having a field day among many well meaning Christians who wrongly hunger for, and seek after, an outward, visible so-called Christian experience. They are in danger of opening themselves up to receive a *"different* [evil] *spirit"* (2 Corinthians 11:4). [2]

The Apostle Paul speaks frankly about the spiritual condition of some Christians in the last days:

> *"The Spirit clearly says that in later times some will* **abandon the faith** *and follow deceiving spirits and things taught by demons."* (Emphasis added)
>
> 1 Timothy 4:1

He goes on to speak about *"Hypocritical liars"* (verse 2) and the sort of things they will teach (verse 3).

While speaking of the general condition and attitude of all people in *"the last days"* (2 Timothy 3:1-5), he goes on to specifically refer to Christians who will turn away from Biblical truth:

> *"For the time will come when* **men will not put up with sound doctrine.** *Instead, to suit their own desires, they will gather around them a great number of teachers to say what their itching ears want to hear.* **They will turn their ears away from the truth** *and turn aside to myths."* (Emphasis added)
>
> 2 Timothy 4:3-4

The Apostle Peter writes similar words in his second letter:

> *"But there were also false prophets among the people, just as there will be* **false teachers among you.** *They will secretly introduce destructive heresies, even denying the sovereign Lord who bought them - bringing swift destruction on themselves.*

*Many will follow their shameful ways and **will bring the way of truth into disrepute**. In their greed these teachers will exploit you with stories they have made up. ...*"
(Emphasis added)

2 Peter 2:1-3

The Lord Jesus Himself warned His disciples of false prophets who would deceive many (Matthew 24:5, 10-11 & 24-25).

All these things we have mentioned are very evident among many churches today and it must surely be signs that His return is very near.

Footnote

---

[1] The truth about Christ's Church and His churches is a subject that we believe has been, and continues to be, neglected and at the very least mismanaged. This author looks into this subject in a separate book, which, if the Lord has not returned, God willing should be available by 2006/07.

[2] If a professing Christian is feeling empty and unfulfilled, and is craving some new (spiritual?) experience, it may be time for them to take stock. They might do well to ask themselves if they have ever been truly born again!

SIGNS OF HIS COMING IN THE WORLD

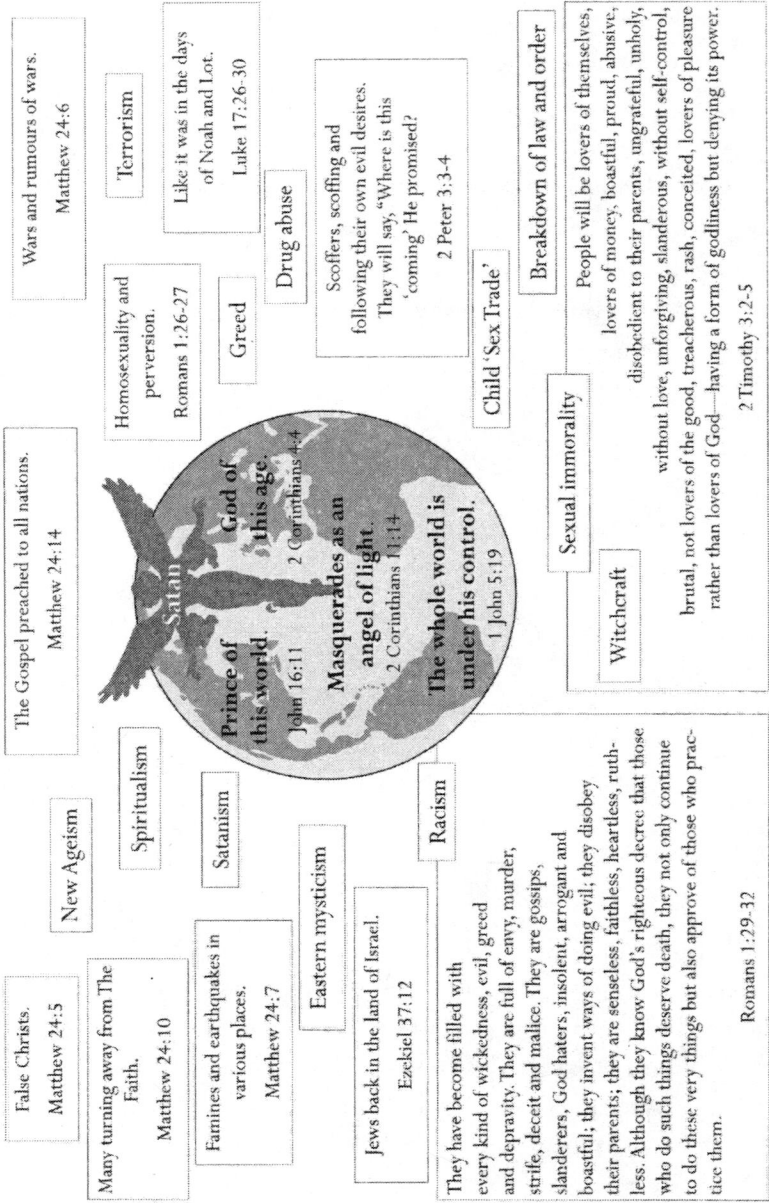

Wars and rumours of wars.
Matthew 24:6

Terrorism

Like it was in the days
of Noah and Lot.
Luke 17:26-30

Drug abuse

Scoffers, scoffing and
following their own evil desires.
They will say, "Where is this
'coming' He promised?
2 Peter 3:3-4

Homosexuality and
perversion.
Romans 1:26-27

Greed

Child 'Sex Trade'

Breakdown of law and order

People will be lovers of themselves,
lovers of money, boastful, proud, abusive,
disobedient to their parents, ungrateful, unholy,
without love, unforgiving, slanderous, without self-control,
brutal, not lovers of the good, treacherous, rash, conceited, lovers of pleasure
rather than lovers of God — having a form of godliness but denying its power.
2 Timothy 3:2-5

The Gospel preached to all nations.
Matthew 24:14

Satan

God of
this age.
2 Corinthians 4:4

Masquerades as an
angel of light.
2 Corinthians 11:14

Prince of
this world.
John 16:11

The whole world is
under his control.
1 John 5:19

Sexual immorality

Witchcraft

New Ageism

Spiritualism

Satanism

Racism

Eastern mysticism

Jews back in the land of Israel.
Ezekiel 37:12

False Christs.
Matthew 24:5

Many turning away from The
Faith.
Matthew 24:10

Famines and earthquakes in
various places.
Matthew 24:7

They have become filled with
every kind of wickedness, evil, greed
and depravity. They are full of envy, murder,
strife, deceit and malice. They are gossips,
slanderers, God haters, insolent, arrogant and
boastful; they invent ways of doing evil; they disobey
their parents; they are senseless, faithless, heartless, ruth-
less. Although they know God's righteous decree that those
who do such things deserve death, they not only continue
to do these very things but also approve of those who prac-
tice them.

Romans 1:29-32

4

Signs of His Coming in the World

It is not commonly understood by many Christians that Christ's Second Advent will involve several separate events. These will occur over a period of several years (and will be considered in later chapters). Many Christians believe that the next event in God's calendar is when Christ will call his Church home to heaven to be with Himself: also, that this event could happen at any moment in time. The events that are associated with the second coming of Christ may cover more years than we might imagine. But the exact day or week, month or year, when God will actually commence this momentous of times is known only to Him.

> *"**No-one knows** about that day or hour, not even the angels in heaven, nor the Son, but only the Father."*
>
> Matthew 24:36

> *"He said to them, '**It is not for you to know** the times or dates the Father has set by His own authority'."*
>
> Acts 1:7

> *"Therefore keep watch, because **you do not know** on what day your Lord will come."*
>
> Matthew 24:42

So, rather than looking for signs of Christ coming for His

Church, we should be looking for the signs of His return to earth to set up His kingdom (pre-empted by His judgments upon earth). These signs lead on to certain specific events that are prophesied in Scripture and will be plain for all the world to see. If the things going on in the world today point to Christ's return to earth, then we can only conclude that the Rapture (see next chapter) is imminent.

Some of the signs in the world that point to the fact we are in the last days are: false Christs; wars and rumours of wars; famines and earthquakes (Matthew 24:5-7); a turning away from the Christian Faith; false prophets; an increase in wickedness (Matthew 24:10-12); an increasing acceptance of homosexuality (Romans 1:24-27); signs in the sun, moon and stars (Luke 21:25); people who are lovers of themselves, lovers of money, boastful, proud, abusive, disobedient to parents, ungrateful, unholy, without love, unforgiving, slanderous, without self control, brutal, treacherous, conceited, lovers of pleasure rather than lovers of God (2 Timothy 3:1-5) and scoffers saying:

> *"Where is this 'coming' He promised?"*
>
> 2 Peter 3:3-4

Besides those things mentioned in the scriptures, noted above, there are many others which indicate a breakdown in society generally. Some of these are: terrorism; drug abuse; child sex trade; adult sex slave trade, witchcraft; Satanism; racism; greed; pornography and the break down of law and order in many places, to name a few.

Incredible though it may sound, there is a school of thought whose adherents teach that Christianity will so spread across the globe that the population in its entirety will eventually become Christian. This couldn't be further from the truth. Nowhere does the Lord suggest this. Quite the opposite, in fact, as the scriptures plainly state. Christianity may be the biggest 'Religion' in the world, but the increase in so-called Christian cults is alarming. The only time we are particularly aware of them is when they rear their ugly heads in the news, usually because of some weird escapade. The Jehovah's Witnesses, Mormons, Masons and Unification Church (Moonies) are among the more commonly known cults whose beliefs, though dressed up like Christianity, are bordering on the Satanic. However, there are hundreds of other little known cults which many innocent victims have been caught up in.

There is increasingly an awareness of and fascination for Eastern religions by people in the west. Many are embracing them. This is particularly true of Islam, which is spreading rapidly in all western countries. Some radical Islamic groups are particularly fanatical, as was made terribly apparent in both New York and Washington on September 11th, 2001.

In the summer of 1999, the NATO forces, including Britain, bombed Serbia and Kosovo, blowing its infrastructure to pieces and killing many innocent people in the process. Meanwhile, Slobodan Milosevic continued systematically to exterminate or banish the ethnic Albanians from Kosovo. More recently, we have seen the military campaign in Afghanistan, and American president George Bush and British Prime Minister Tony Blair's war against Iraq to oust Saddam Hussein and his evil regime. So what's new? Nothing really! It's just that there are many more wars and rumours of wars and killings going on in the world than there have been before. The Bible tells us that it's going to get far worse. When the Lord referred to such things, as we see going on in the world, He said they were the beginning of birth-pains.

> *"You will hear of wars and rumours of wars, but see to it that you are not alarmed. Such things must happen, but the end is still to come. Nation will rise against nation, and kingdom against kingdom. There will be famines and earthquakes in various places. **All these are the beginning of birth pains.**"* (Emphasis added)
>
> Matthew 24:6-8

If these are *"the beginning of birth pains"*, what will it be like for the population of the earth when "the end" comes and the Day of the Lord has arrived?

Another phenomenon on the increase in the world today is the belief in beings from outer space. Many who have looked into this phenomenon believe that this is yet another of the Devil's deceptions in leading people away from God's truth, and are convinced that these so-called sightings of alien creatures and their craft are in fact demonic in origin. It is believed that they are manifested in the same way as are ghosts and ghostly apparitions which, besides appearance, can also include touch, smell and levitation besides the usual sights and sounds. It is interesting to note that many advocates of aliens from outer space believe, or have been involved in Spiritualism or the Occult.

The increase in natural disasters, earthquakes and famines around the world are also very alarming and these, as the last scripture quotation suggests, are again signs that point to the fact that our Lord Jesus Christ could be coming soon. But surely one of the greatest signs of all has to be that the Jews are back in the land of Israel. As far back as the days of Moses, God has foretold of the things which we are witnessing in our days. One would think that perhaps some high level openly Christian politicians would take notice of what has been written by God in His word and at least consider the implications.

> *"...Then the Lord your God will restore your fortunes and have compassion on you and **gather you again from all the nations** where He scattered you. Even if you have been banished to the utmost distant land under the heavens, from there **the Lord your God will gather you and bring you back**. He will bring you to the land that belonged to your fathers and you will take possession of it."* (Emphasis added)
>
> Deuteronomy 30:3-5

> *"Therefore prophesy and say to them: 'This is what the sovereign LORD says: O my people, I am going to open your graves and bring you up from them; **I will bring you back to the land of Israel.**'"* (Emphasis added)
>
> Ezekiel 37:12

There are many other scriptures that speak specifically of God bringing his people back to the land of Israel and, as a nation, Israel is back in the land. However, they are there in unbelief. Though a growing number of Jews do believe in Jesus, both in Israel and around the world, the nation as a whole, still does not accept that Jesus is their Messiah. Sadly, their spiritual blindness continues to this day and they will suffer many things before they finally accept Jesus as their Messiah King and are saved.

"How awful that day will be! None will be like it. It will be a time of trouble for Jacob [nation of Israel], **but he will be saved out of it.**" (Emphasis added)

Jeremiah 30:7

*"And so **all Israel will be saved,** as it is written: 'The deliverer will come from Zion; He will turn godlessness away from Jacob. And this is My covenant with them when I take away their sins.'"* (Emphasis added)

Romans 11:26-27

When we see all of these things in the world beginning to come together piece by piece, surely we should sit up and take note of it, for Jesus said:

*"'When these things **begin to take place,** stand up and lift up your heads, because your redemption is drawing near.' ... He told them this parable: 'Look at the fig-tree and all the trees. When they sprout leaves, you can see for yourselves and know that summer is near. Even so, **when you see these things happening,** you know that the kingdom of God is near.'"* (Emphasis added)

Luke 21:28-31

THE RESSURECTION AND RAPTURE

For the Lord Himself will come down from heaven, with a loud command, with the voice of the archangel and with the trumpet call of God.

1 Thessalonians 4:16

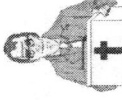

The gospel of the Kingdom preached in the whole world, then the end will come.

Matthew 24:14

Those who have died, unsaved, will remain in death for another one thousand years.

Revelation 20:5

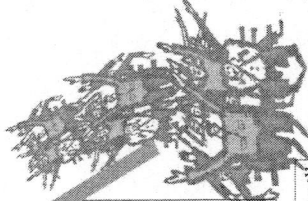

And so we will be with the Lord for ever.

1 Thessalonians 4:17

After that, we who are still alive and are left will be caught up together with them in the clouds to meet the Lord in the air.

1 Thessalonians 4:17

For the trumpet will sound, the dead will be raised imperishable, and we will be changed. ...Then the saying that is written will come true: "Death has been swallowed up in victory."

1 Corinthians 15:52-54

I will come back and take you to be with me that you also may be where I am.

John 14:3

The trumpet will sound.

1 Corinthians 15:52

The dead in Christ will rise first.

1 Thessalonians 4:16

And after my skin has been destroyed, yet in my flesh I will see God. ...
If a man dies, will he live again? All the days of my hard service I will wait for my renewal to come. You will call and I will answer You; You will long for the creature Your hands have made.

Job 19:26/14:14-15

5

The Resurrection and Rapture

The word 'Rapture' is not found anywhere in the Bible but is taken from the Latin word *RAPERE* which in turn is translated from the Greek word *HARPAZO*, meaning 'to seize', and is translated 'caught up' in 1 Thessalonians 4:17. It has been universally accepted as referring to that event, longed for by Christians down the centuries, when the Lord Jesus will return and take the Church, His Bride, to be with Himself in Heaven as He promised:

> *"Do not let your hearts be troubled. Trust in God, trust also in Me. In My Fathers house are many rooms; if it were not so, I would have told you. I am going there to prepare a place for you. And if I go and prepare a place for you, **I will come back** and **take you to be with Me** that you also may be where I am."* (Emphasis added)
>
> John 14:1-3

All living Christians will participate in the rapture when the Lord Jesus returns for His Church. Christians who have died, whose souls have gone to be with Jesus in heaven, will be raised from the dead.

> *"Brothers, we do not want you to be ignorant about those who fall asleep, or to grieve like the rest of men, who have no hope. We believe that Jesus died and rose again and so we believe that*

51

God will bring with Jesus those who have fallen asleep [i.e. died] *in Him. According to the Lord's own word, we tell you that we who are still alive, who are left till the coming of the Lord, will certainly not precede those who have fallen asleep* [died]. *For the Lord Himself will come down from Heaven, with a loud command, with the voice of the archangel and with the trumpet call of God, and* **the dead in Christ will rise first** [the resurrection]. *After that* **we who are still alive** *and are left* **will be caught up** [harpazó - the rapture] *together with them in the clouds to meet the Lord in the air. And so we will be with the Lord for ever."* (Emphasis added)

1 Thessalonians 4:13-17

"Listen, I tell you a mystery: We will not all sleep [die], *but we will all be changed - in a flash, in the twinkling of an eye, at the last trumpet. For the trumpet will sound,* **the dead will be raised imperishable, and we will be changed**. *For the perishable must clothe itself with the imperishable, and the mortal with immortality."* (Emphasis added)

1 Corinthians 15:51-53

Jesus was referring to this event when He said to Martha,

"I am the resurrection and the life. He who believes in Me will live, even though he dies [the resurrection of those who have died in Jesus]; *and whoever lives and believes in Me* [when I come again] *will never die* [the rapture]. *Do you believe this?"*

John 11:25-26

The new resurrected or changed bodies of Christians

will be just like our Lord Jesus' body after He was raised from the dead. We are all born with a natural, earthly, sinful, perishable body, but when the trumpet of the Lord sounds, all Christians, those who have died and those living, will be called immediately into His presence and will be given new, immortal, imperishable, sinless, spiritual, glorious, heavenly bodies!

"So it will be with the resurrection of the dead. The body that is sown is perishable, it is raised imperishable; it is sown in dishonour, it is raised in glory; it is sown in weakness, it is raised in power; it is sown a natural body, it is raised a spiritual body.

If there is a natural body, there is also a spiritual body. So it is written: 'The first man Adam became a living being'; the last Adam [Christ] a life-giving spirit. The spiritual did not come first, but the natural, and after that the spiritual. The first man [Adam] was of the dust of the earth, the second Man [Christ] from heaven. As was the earthly man [Adam], so are those who are of the earth [everyone]; and as is the Man from heaven, so also are those who are of heaven [Christians]. And just as we [Christians] have borne the likeness of the earthly man, so shall we bear the likeness of the Man from heaven."

1 Corinthians 15:42-49

"But our [Christians] citizenship is in heaven. And we eagerly await a Saviour from there, the Lord Jesus Christ, who, by the power that enables Him to bring everything under His control, will transform our lowly bodies so that they will be like His glorious body."

Philippians 3:20-21

There are some Christians who (in our view) mistakenly believe that the Church is to remain on earth when God pours out His wrath and judges the world. It is our belief that the scriptures clearly do not teach this. However, there will be many people who become Christians after the Resurrection/Rapture, who will be here on earth during the time of the Antichrist and God's judgement on earth (as we shall see later). It is this fact that seems to cause some confusion.

Paul had to write to the Christians at Thessalonica to reassure them that the troubles they were having to endure at that time were not because the day of the Lord had come as some were saying.

> *"Now we beseech you brethren by the coming of our Lord Jesus Christ and by our gathering together unto Him,* [i.e. the Resurrection/Rapture] *that ye be not soon shaken in mind, or be troubled, neither by spirit, nor by word, nor by letter as from us, as that the day of Christ is at hand. Let no man deceive you by any means: for that day shall not come except there come a falling away*[1] *first, and that man of sin* [Antichrist] *be revealed, the son of perdition."*
>
> 2 Thessalonians 2:1-3 (AV)

Likewise, confusion, in our day, has come about by the misunderstanding of certain scriptures. We can be assured that God has every intention of taking His Church out of the world before He pours out His wrath and judgement on it. This is what God says in His Word:

(Where '*' equals Christians who belong to *"the Church, which is*

His body" Ephesians 122b-23a)

- 'We* shall be saved from God's wrath.   Romans 5:9

- 'Jesus, who rescues us* from the coming wrath'.   1 Thessalonians 1:10

- 'God did not appoint us* to suffer wrath but to receive salvation'.   1 Thessalonians 5:9

- 'God chose you* to be saved through the sanctifying work of the Spirit'.   2 Thessalonians 2:13

- 'He will appear a second time to bring salvation to those* waiting for Him'.   Hebrews 9:28

Noah and his family were rescued from the flood by being safe in the Ark before God's judgement fell (Genesis 6:9-7:23). Lot was taken out of Sodom before God's judgement rained down on it (Genesis 19:12-25). We are told,

> *"It will be just like this on the day the Son of Man is revealed."*
> Luke 17:30

Every single Christian who is alive when Jesus comes for His Church will be taken. His Bride will be complete and He will call her to be with Himself.

> *"Listen, I tell you a mystery: We will not all sleep, but we will all be changed - in a flash, in the twinkling of an eye, at the last trumpet. For the trumpet will sound, the dead will be raised imperishable, and we will be changed."*
>
> 1 Corinthians 15:51-52

Those who are not Christians will be left behind.

It seemed to be taken for granted in the early days of the Church that the expected Rapture would be sudden and could happen at any time:

> *"But you, brothers, are not in darkness so that this day should surprise you like a thief."*
>
> 1 Thessalonians 5:4

It will, however, surprise, shock and confound all those who are left behind, and bring terror and panic to the whole world, especially to those who think they are Christians but are not!

It might be as well to note here, that there seems to be a suggestion by the Apostle Paul that the Resurrection/Rapture is allied with God taking up and dealing with Israel, in a special way, as a nation again.

> *"For if their [Israel's] rejection is the reconciliation of the world, what will their acceptance be but life from the dead?"*
>
> Romans 11:15

With no Christians left on earth because the Church has

been taken to heaven, the restraining influence of the Holy Spirit among the nations against evil (and the faith and testimony about Jesus Christ by God's people) will have been removed from the world. There will no longer be anything to prevent the lawless one (known as the Antichrist) from being revealed.

> *"For the secret power of lawlessness is already at work; but the one who now holds it back will continue to do so till he is taken out of the way. Then the lawless one will be revealed, whom the Lord Jesus will overthrow with the breath of His mouth and destroy by the splendour of His coming."* (That is, when He returns to earth. See Revelation 19:11-21)
>
> 2 Thessalonians 2:7-8

It is evident that when God speaks about *"The Day of the LORD"*, He is actually speaking about a period of several years. He will pour out His wrath and judgement upon the nations of the earth during this time. Here are some Scriptures that speak about that day (Emphasis has been added):

> *"See, **the day of the LORD** is coming - a cruel day, with wrath and fierce anger - to make the land desolate and destroy the sinners within it."*
>
> Isaiah 13:9

> *"For the day is near, **the day of the LORD** is near - a day of clouds, a time of doom for the nations."*
>
> Ezekiel 30:3

> *"Alas for that day! For **the day of the LORD** is near: it will*

come like destruction from the Almighty."

Joel 1:15

*"**The day of the LORD** is near for all nations. As you have done, it will be done to you; your deeds will return upon your own head."*

Obadiah 1:15

*"But **the day of the Lord** will come like a thief. The heavens will disappear with a roar; the elements will be destroyed by fire, and the earth and everything in it will be laid bare."*

2 Peter 3:10

It would appear that *"the day of the LORD"* will be ushered in at the time of the Rapture/Resurrection of Christ's Church or very soon after. The completion of it will be when Jesus returns to earth in heavenly glory, judges those still living among the nations and sets up His earthly Kingdom (Matthew 25:31-46 & Revelation 11:15-17 & 19:4-6). In the broader sense, it would include His one thousand year reign.

When Jesus left this earth and went back into heaven it was in full view of His disciples, from the Mount of Olives, just east of Jerusalem. When He returns to earth it will be to this same place and in full view.

*"... This same Jesus, who has been taken from you into heaven, will come back **in the same way** you have seen Him go into heaven."* (Emphasis added)

Acts 1:11b

"Then the Lord will go out and fight against those nations, as

He fights in the day of battle. On that day His feet will stand on the Mount of Olives, east of Jerusalem, and the Mount of Olives will be split in two from east to west, forming a great valley, with half of the mountain moving north and half moving south."

Zechariah 14:3-4

Footnote

---

[1] More accurately '... except the departure come ...' from the Greek *APOSTASIA* or *APOSTASION* meaning 'departure' or 'divorce'. It may be of interest to know that the early translations of the Bible into English, such as the Wycliff, Tyndale, and Coverdale Bibles, translated this word "departing". In the context of what the Apostle Paul is saying here, i.e., *"our being gathered to Him"* (v.1), I believe *APOSTASIA*, "the departure", can only be referring to "the departure" of the Church to heaven and not to the spiritual condition of Christians just prior to the Lord's return for His Church. Although the Apostle does speak about the spiritual and moral condition of the unsaved in 2 Thessalonians (e.g., ch.1:8 & 2:10b-12), nowhere does he specifically talk about the spiritual condition of believers just prior to Christ's return for His Church. That subject is dealt with elsewhere in the scriptures (ex. 1 Timothy 4:1-3, 2 Timothy 4:3-4 & 2 Peter 2:1-3 etc. See also chapter 3).

Note: In 2 Thessalonians 2:3, the NIV translates *"APOSTASIA"* as *"the rebellion"*. I believe this translation to be wrong. The translators may have had in mind either the spiritual/moral condition of the unsaved population of the world becoming worse or Christians rebelling against God's word. But again, though it is obvious to many that things are rapidly deteriorating in the world and that many Christians are giving up much of God's truth, it is verse 1 that gives us the context: *"our* [the Church] *being **gathered to Him"*** !

FROM THE RAPTURE TO CHRIST'S RETURN TO EARTH

The Christians who were resurrected and Raptured into heaven now appear before the judgment seat of Christ and receive their rewards.

2 Corinthians 5:10 / 1 Corinthians 3:11-15 & 4:5

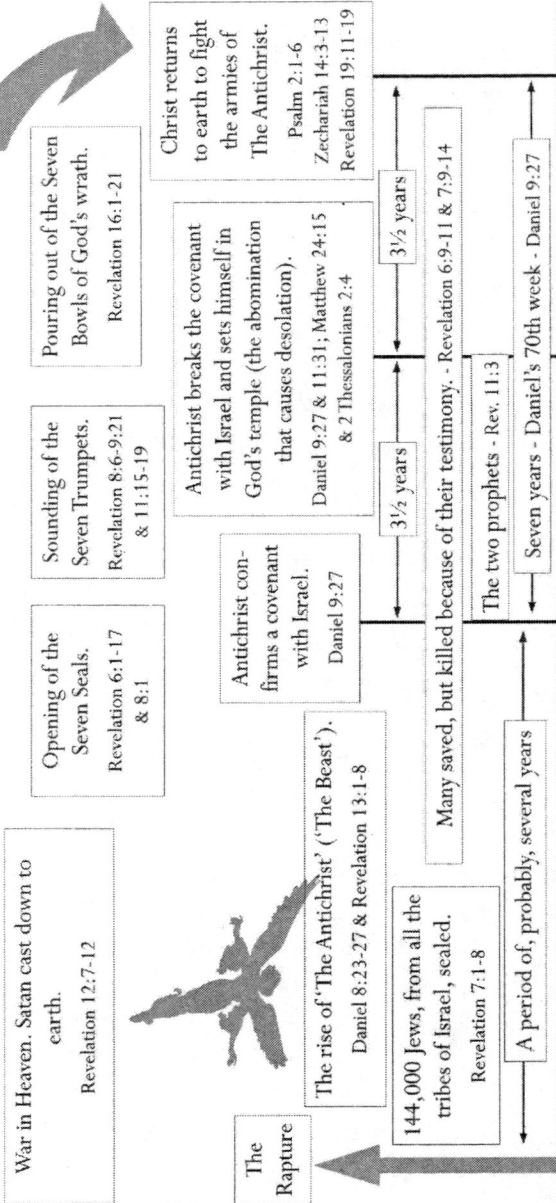

War in Heaven. Satan cast down to earth.
Revelation 12:7-12

The rise of 'The Antichrist' ('The Beast').
Daniel 8:23-27 & Revelation 13:1-8

The Rapture

144,000 Jews, from all the tribes of Israel, sealed.
Revelation 7:1-8

Opening of the Seven Seals.
Revelation 6:1-17 & 8:1

Sounding of the Seven Trumpets.
Revelation 8:6-9:21 & 11:15-19

Pouring out of the Seven Bowls of God's wrath.
Revelation 16:1-21

Christ returns to earth to fight the armies of The Antichrist.
Psalm 2:1-6
Zechariah 14:3-13
Revelation 19:11-19

Antichrist breaks the covenant with Israel and sets himself in God's temple (the abomination that causes desolation).
Daniel 9:27 & 11:31; Matthew 24:15 & 2 Thessalonians 2:4

Antichrist confirms a covenant with Israel.
Daniel 9:27

Many saved, but killed because of their testimony. - Revelation 6:9-11 & 7:9-14

The two prophets - Rev. 11:3

A period of, probably, several years

3½ years

3½ years

Seven years - Daniel's 70th week - Daniel 9:27

There are so many prophecies in the Old and New Testaments about this period of time that it would be impossible to quote or refer to all of them here. The ones chosen aim to cover the main events. There has to be a period of time before Daniel's 'Seventieth Week' to account for the rise of Antichrist and the establishment of his confederate kingdom. He has to be already in power when, at the beginning of Daniel's 'Seventieth Week', he confirms a covenant with Israel.

6

From the Rapture
to Christ's Return to Earth

There have been many disagreements and controversies about the period between the Rapture and Christ's return. So many fantastic and sometimes ridiculous interpretations have been given about the things prophesied for this time that it is enough to leave the average Christian in a complete mental 'fuzz'. There are many prophecies in the Bible about the days just prior to Jesus' return to earth, and the judgement of God on the world of unbelievers, and many of them are hard to understand. It will probably be far easier for those people who are saved during those terrible days to understand these prophecies than it is for Christians alive today. However, it is still possible for us to understand much of what is contained in them.

One must be careful not to read into the prophecies something that is not there; and on the other hand, not to read out of them something that is. The misinterpretations and confusion about these prophetic events are probably born out of the fact that even many Christians cannot, or will not, accept at face value the amazing and incredible things that God is saying. They are like Israel, as a nation, who could not accept what God was doing when Jesus first came to earth from heaven to suffer and die for the sins of the world, and who generally still do not accept the prophecies concerning the rejection and suffering of their Messiah King.

"For He [God] has set a day when He will judge the world with justice by the Man He has appointed. He has given proof of this to all men by raising Him from the dead."

Acts 17:31

"By the same word the present heavens and earth are reserved for fire, being kept for the day of judgement and destruction of ungodly men."

2 Peter 3:7

"For then there will be great distress, unequalled from the beginning of the world until now - and never to be equalled again."

Matthew 24:21

There seems to be an attitude in the world that tends to disregard warnings of disaster and impending doom. In Noah's day, God destroyed the world that then was, and only Noah and his wife and his three sons and their wives were saved. It is evident that God the Holy Spirit spoke through Noah to warn of the coming judgment, but that no-one believed Noah's preaching (1 Peter 3:19). We are plainly told that God did not spare the world that existed then because of the people's ungodliness and wickedness and their evil hearts (2 Peter 2:5 & Genesis 6:5).

Those who think that the flood of Noah's day is only a story should remember that the Lord Jesus endorsed the flood as fact and likened the last days just prior to His return to earth to the days just prior to the judgment of God in Noah's day. Life seemed to go on without anyone taking any interest in the God who created all things. Everyone lived their own lives and cared less about anything else - until the judgment fell!

Jesus goes on to tell of the situation in Sodom and the surrounding cities, whose ungodliness brought down the judgment of God on them also (see Genesis 18:16-19:29). Here's what Jesus said:

> *"Just as it was in the days of Noah, so also will it be in the days of the Son of Man. People were eating, drinking, marrying and being given in marriage up to the day Noah entered the ark. Then the flood came and destroyed them all. It was the same in the days of Lot. People were eating and drinking, buying and selling, planting and building. But the day Lot left Sodom, fire and sulfur rained down from heaven and destroyed them all.* **It will be just like this on the day the Son of Man is revealed.***"* (Emphasis added)

Luke 17:26-30

(See also Matthew 24:37-39)

Who would have believed the destruction and death of the first and second world wars if someone had foretold such happenings? Who believed that such genocide would ever take place in former Yugoslavia during the last decade of the twentieth century? Apparently, there were warnings about a possible terrorist strike in America before September 11th 2001, but did anyone believe such warnings so as to act positively on them?

In the Bible, God tells us of the judgement that must surely come upon a world of sinful people who are bent on destroying each other and the world in which we live, who refuse to give God any credit for His power and authority and have little or no reverence and respect for His majesty. Yet this same Lord God, in His grace, mercy and loving kindness, waits patiently for sinners to repent and believe the Gospel so that they may be saved from their sins and the judgement to come.

> *"The Lord is not slow in keeping His promise, as some understand slowness. He is patient with you, **not wanting anyone to perish**, but everyone to come to repentance."* (Emphasis added)
>
> 2 Peter 3:9

After the Rapture, 144,000 Jews will be sealed as servants of God, and millions of other people from every nation will be saved.

> *"Then I heard the number of those who were sealed: 144,000 from all the tribes of Israel."*
>
> Revelation 7:4

> *"After this I looked and there before me was a great multitude that no one could count, from every nation, tribe, people and language, standing before the throne and in front of the Lamb* [Christ]. ... *These are they who have come out of the great tribulation; they have washed their robes and made them white in the blood of the Lamb."*
>
> Revelation 7:9-14

This will most probably be because of the many people who heard of the coming again of the Lord Jesus before the Rapture but who had never trusted Him for salvation. When millions of people suddenly disappear from all over the world (the Rapture) they will put two and two together, believe the

Gospel and accept Jesus Christ as their Saviour. They will then proclaim salvation through Christ and warn of the things about to come upon the world. These Christians will suffer persecution and death for their faith.

"Then you will be handed over to be persecuted and put to death, and you will be hated by all nations because of Me."

Matthew 24:9

"... And I saw the souls of those who had been beheaded because of their testimony for Jesus and because of the word of God. They had not worshipped the beast or his image and had not received his mark on their foreheads or their hands. They came to life and reigned with Christ for a thousand years."

Revelation 20:4

Those who knew the Gospel before the Rapture, but who rejected Jesus as Saviour and continually refuse to believe God's truth, will be condemned and perish.

"... They perish because they refused to love the truth and so be saved. For this reason God sends them a powerful delusion so that they will believe the lie [Antichrist].*"*

2 Thessalonians 2:10-11

Satan and his angels presently have access to heaven as well as earth, but after the Rapture there will be a war in heaven in which God's angels will overcome Satan and his angels and cast them out of heaven down to earth (Revelation 12:7-9). This will be a terrible time for those living on earth.

"Therefore rejoice, you heavens and you who dwell in them! But woe to the earth and the sea, because the Devil has gone down to you! He is filled with fury, because he knows that his time is short."

Revelation 12:12

During those years between the Rapture and Christ's return to earth, there will be war and famine and such devastation that the Lord Jesus tells us:

"If those days had not been cut short, no-one would survive, but for the sake of the elect those days will be shortened."

Matthew 24:22

This will be the time of God's wrath and judgement against the world for its wickedness and its rejection of Jesus Christ and His offer of mercy and forgiveness. It is during this time that the Antichrist (referred to in some places as the Beast) will arise and establish a confederate kingdom made up of ten nations. Together, they will seek to fight against the Lord Jesus.

"The ten horns you saw are ten kings who have not yet received a kingdom, but who for one hour will receive authority as kings along with the beast. They will have one purpose and will give their power and authority to the beast. They will make war against the Lamb, but the Lamb will overcome them because He is Lord of lords and King of kings - and with Him will be His called, chosen and faithful followers."

Revelation 17:12-14

The Beast, or Antichrist, will at first seem to be

sympathetic to the nation of Israel and confirm a covenant with them for seven years. Exactly what this covenant is no one can be sure but it will, no doubt, be a significant political arrangement with Israel in which they will be completely fooled. The Antichrist's intent is to deceive them, for after three and a half years he will break the covenant and seek to destroy them. He has another purpose as well. It is to fight against the Lord Jesus Christ, and the armies of heaven, when He returns to earth in judgment and to set up His kingdom.

> *"He* [Antichrist] *will confirm a covenant with many for one 'seven' [seven years]. In the middle of the 'seven' he will put an end to sacrifice and offering. And on a wing of the temple he will set up an abomination that causes desolation, until the end that is decreed is poured out on him."*
>
> Daniel 9:27

> *"He* [Antichrist] *was given power to make war against the saints and to conquer them. And he was given authority over every tribe, people, language and nation."*
>
> Revelation 13:7

> *"Then I saw the beast and the kings of the earth and their armies gathered together to make war against the Rider* [Christ] *on the horse and His army."*
>
> Revelation 19:19

Allowing suitable time for the rise of the Antichrist to political leadership and to establish his kingdom, let's say a few years, plus Daniel's seven years, we are looking at something in the region of at least ten years, maybe more, between the

Rapture and Christ's return to earth.

At the end, Jesus Himself will return with the armies of heaven to the Mount of Olives, and destroy the Antichrist and the armies of the nations:

> *"Then the Lord will go out and fight against those nations, as He fights in the day of battle. On that day His feet will stand on the Mount of Olives, east of Jerusalem and the Mount of Olives will be split in two from east to west, forming a great valley, with half of the mountain moving north and half moving south. You will flee by my mountain valley, for it will extend to Azel. You will flee as you fled from the earthquake in the days of Uzziah king of Judah. Then the Lord my God will come, and all the holy ones with him."*
>
> Zechariah 14:3-5

It would be difficult to put a number on the people that die in those days of God's wrath and judgment, but we know that there will be few people left on the earth when Jesus returns to set up His kingdom. It makes solemn reading:

> *"Therefore a curse consumes the earth; its people must bear their guilt. Therefore earth's inhabitants are burned up, and **very few are left***." (Emphasis added)
>
> Isaiah 24:6

The Lord Jesus will then gather before Him all the peoples of the nations who are left on the earth and divide them like a shepherd divides the sheep and the goats. Those who are saved (the sheep) will enter into His Kingdom on Earth. The unsaved (the goats) will be cast out into eternal punishment (Matthew 25:31-46).

THE BEAST OR ANTICHRIST

The coming of the lawless one will be in accordance with the work of Satan displayed in all kinds of counterfeit miracles, signs and wonders, and in every sort of evil that deceives those who are perishing.

2 Thessalonians 2:9-10

He will speak against the Most High and oppress His saints and try to change the set times and laws. The saints [Christians] will be handed over to him for a time, times and half a time [3½ years].

Daniel 7:25

... He will exalt and magnify himself above every god and will say unheard-of things against the God of gods. He will be successful until the time of wrath is completed, for what has been determined must take place.

Daniel 11:36

He will become very strong, but not by his own power. He will cause astounding devastation and will succeed in whatever he does. He will destroy the mighty men and the holy people. He will cause deceit to prosper, and he will consider himself superior. When they feel secure, he will destroy many and take his stand against the Prince of princes [Christ]. Yet he will be destroyed, but not by human power.

Daniel 8:24-25

... He will invade many countries and sweep through them like a flood. He will also invade the Beautiful Land [Israel]. Many countries will fall, but Edom, Moab and the leaders of Ammon will be delivered from his hand. He will extend his power over many countries; Egypt will not escape.

Daniel 11:40-42

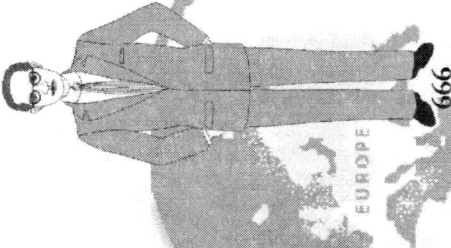

He also forced everyone, small and great, rich and poor, free and slave, to receive a mark on his right hand or on his forehead, so that no-one could buy or sell unless he had the mark, which is the name of the beast or the number of his name. This calls for wisdom. If anyone has insight, let him calculate the number of the beast, for it is man's number. His number is 666.

Revelation 13:16-18

7

The Beast or Antichrist

The intention here is only to touch on a few key points about the Antichrist. It is generally agreed that, according to 2 Thessalonians 2:6-8, he will not be revealed till after the Church has been taken to heaven (the Resurrection/Rapture). So to point the finger at any current political or religious figure is a waste of time. A key point we note from scripture is that:

"... The dragon [Satan] *gave the beast* [Antichrist] *his power and his throne and great authority."*

Revelation 13:2

He once used this to tempt Jesus in the desert.

"And he said to Him, 'I will give You all their authority and splendour, for it has been given to me, and I can give it to anyone I want to.'"

Luke 4:6

It may be that Satan enters, possesses and takes control of the Antichrist, as he did Judas when he betrayed the Lord (John 13:27). Satan, having been cast out of heaven (Revelation 12:7-9), is going to need the physical means to operate in a physical world. Possessing someone's body is the logical way of doing just that. Hence the Antichrist's coming is described as being:

"... in accordance with the work of Satan, displayed in all kinds of counterfeit miracles, signs and wonders, and in every sort of evil that deceives those who are perishing"

2 Thessalonians 2:9-10

His power comes from Satan himself and, incredibly, most of the people on the earth will willingly follow him and even worship him!

"... The whole world was astonished and followed the beast. Men worshipped the dragon because he had given authority to the beast, and they also worshipped the beast ... All the inhabitants of the earth will worship the beast ..."

Revelation 13:3-4 & 8

One noticeable feature of the Antichrist is that he receives an apparent fatal wound from a sword and yet lives. If the foolish and worthless shepherd spoken of by Zechariah is the same person, then the wound involves his arm and right eye. In which case he will be easily recognisable.

"... Whose fatal wound had been healed." "... who was wounded by the sword and yet lived."

Revelation 13:12 & 14

"Woe to the worthless shepherd, who deserts the flock! May the sword strike his arm and his right eye! May his arm be completely withered, his right eye totally blinded!"

Zechariah 11:17

Another feature of the Antichrist is his 'sidekick', a

religiously motivated false prophet who has an image of the Antichrist set up and who forces all people to worship it. Those who don't are killed! (If that sounds familiar, see Daniel 3:1-7). He also forces everyone to receive the mark or number of the beast, without which no one can buy or sell anything.

> *"Then I saw another beast, coming out of the earth. He had two horns like a lamb, but he spoke like a dragon. He exercised all the authority of the first beast on his behalf, and made the earth and its inhabitants to worship the first beast. ... He also forced everyone, small and great, rich and poor, free and slave, to receive a mark on his right hand or forehead, so that no one could buy or sell unless he had the mark, which is the name of the beast or the number of his name. ... His number is 666."*
>
> Revelation 13:11-18

There is very little foundation for the idea that the Antichrist rises out of Italy and that his kingdom will be part of the area which is now the EEC, as conjectured by some Christians.

The EEC 'thing' was popular when there were less than ten countries involved. Those who pushed the idea thought it would stop when it got to ten (the ten kings of Daniel 7:24 and Revelation 17:12-13), but again, they are loath to let it go even now that the EEC has increased to well past ten countries! This idea is based mainly on Daniel 2 concerning the statue whose legs were of iron, representing the Roman Empire, and the feet and ten toes that were made of iron and clay, representing the Antichrist's kingdom.

The interpretation is clear: The kingdom, as represented by the iron and clay, is characterised by not only having the strength of the iron (the Roman Empire was very large, brutal and cruel, which will be one of the characteristics of the Antichrist's regime), but also weakness and instability, represented by the clay.

Another scripture that is used to promote the idea that the Antichrist arises out of a revived Roman Empire is Daniel 9:26-27. Here, it reveals the fact that the Messiah will be killed:

"... the Anointed One will be cut off ..."

and that

"The people of the ruler who will come will destroy the city [Jerusalem] *and the sanctuary* [the temple]" verse 26.

It is admitted that verses 26 and 27 are difficult to translate from the original language and thereby cloud the issue somewhat. But the 'people' here referred to can only be the Romans, and the 'ruler', under whom they destroyed Jerusalem, was the Emperor Vespasian, AD 69-79. It was Vespasian's son, Titus, who led the Roman army against the Jews in AD 70, and fulfilled what God, through Daniel, had foretold. Vespasian was not there personally, but his 'people' were. The 'Revived Roman Empire' school of thought says that 'the ruler' of verse 26 is the Antichrist. We do not believe this to be correct. Rather, it is reading into it something that is just not there, an idea that merely suits the theory. Furthermore, the statement in its entirety cannot be referring to Antichrist, for scripture does not say that the Antichrist will destroy Jerusalem, or the Sanctuary (Temple); only that he, along with other nations, are gathered by God to 'fight against it' and capture it (Zechariah 14:2). Indeed, 2 Thessalonians 2:4 tells us that Antichrist (the *"man of lawlessness"*, verse 3), sets himself up in the Temple at Jerusalem, proclaiming to be God. So he cannot both destroy it and sit in it at one and the same time!

Though there is no break made by the translators, in the text of Daniel's ninth chapter after the word 'sanctuary' in verse 26, there should be, because reference is made immediately to 'the end', and speaks of 'war' that will continue to 'the end.' This can only be referring to 'the end' of this age in the context given. The 'he' of verse 27 is obviously the Antichrist because of what follows.[1]

We believe Daniel 9:26-27 should be written with pauses between the sentences like this (comments in [brackets] are to aid the understanding):

"After the sixty-two 'sevens', the Anointed One [Christ] *will be cut off* [crucified] *and will have nothing.*

The people [the Romans] *of the ruler who will come* [the then future ruler Emperor Vespasian] *will destroy the city and the sanctuary* [Jerusalem and the temple].

The end [of this present age] *will come like a flood: War will continue until the end* [when Christ returns to earth], *and desolations have been decreed. He* [Antichrist] *will confirm a covenant with many* [in Israel] *for one 'seven'* [seven years]. *In the middle of the 'seven' he* [Antichrist] *will put an end to sacrifice and offering* [in the rebuilt Temple at Jerusalem]. *And on a wing of the temple he will set up an abomination that causes desolation* [an image, Revelation 13:14-15], *until the end that is decreed is poured out on him."*

There is no doubt that the kingdom of the Antichrist will cover some of the area that belonged to the Roman Empire. That Empire stretched from Britain and Western Europe right across to North Africa, in the south, and over much of what is now referred to as the Middle East, and beyond.

If we consider Daniel 8:19-26, we can only conclude that Antichrist's kingdom must also cover, at least in part, the area of the kingdoms of Media and Persia, Greece (under Alexander the Great) and the four smaller kingdoms (under Seleucus, Cassander, Ptolemy and Lysimachus) that emerged after Alexander's early death in 323 BC. From their kingdoms comes one who is described as *"a stern faced king, a master of intrigue"* (verse 23). We are told that this king takes his stand against the Prince of princes (Jesus Christ) and is ultimately destroyed, *"but not by human power"* (verse 25). This 'stern faced king' and 'master of intrigue' has to be the 'Antichrist' or 'Beast', and can only be referring to that event described in 2 Thessalonians 2:8 and Revelation 19:20.

So why is there no mention or implication of the Roman Empire here? Simply because there is more to the Antichrist's kingdom than just the idea of a "Revived Roman Empire"!

We are told that he is to be given authority over every tribe, people, language and nation, and that the whole world will worship the beast (Revelation 13:7-8). So we cannot be complacent as to his power and influence.

Other descriptive characteristics of the Antichrist's kingdom are as a leopard (the Grecian Empire), indicative of swiftness to conquer; a bear (the Medo Persian Empire), indicative of power and strength; and a lion (the Babylonian Empire), indicative of intelligence and regal splendour (Revelation 13:2 with Daniel 7:4-6).

All of these characteristics **together** indicate what sort of kingdom and rule the Antichrist will have.

Another reason for discounting a "Revived Roman Empire" is to take note of what the angel said to John in Revelation chapter 17. Here, John is shown a woman riding a beast. This beast represents a king, the Antichrist, and his kingdom.

John is told:

"The beast which you saw, once was, now is not, and will come up out of the Abyss and go to his destruction. The inhabitants of the earth whose names have not been written in the book of life from the creation of the world will be astonished when they see the beast, because he once was, now is not, and yet will come."

Revelation 17:8

Notice that the angel tells John that the beast *"once was, **now is not**, and yet will come"*. This must rule out the idea that the beast's kingdom is a Revived Roman Empire, for the empire in John's day was most definitely Roman! The angel tells John it ***"now is not"***! So if the beast existed before, but did not exist during John's lifetime, he cannot be of Roman origin.

As for those who speculate that the woman riding the beast is Rome (more particularly, the Roman Catholic Church), again, they are surely just accommodating the "Revived Roman Empire" theory. Indeed, we are told in verse 5 of the same chapter that the woman has a title written on her forehead:

"MYSTERY
BABYLON THE GREAT

*THE MOTHER OF PROSTITUTES
AND OF THE ABOMINATIONS OF THE EARTH."*

Babylon is an ancient city almost as old as time itself. Its location today is just east of the Euphrates River, 90 km (56 miles) south of Baghdad, Iraq. It was founded by Nimrod, (Genesis 10:8-10) and the place where, because of mans disobedience, God introduced a multi-language world (Genesis 11:1-9). It was the place to which God had the people of Israel taken into captivity for seventy years because of their sin (2 Chronicles 36:15-21).

So here, having been extensively rebuilt by Saddam Hussein during the 1980s and 90s, Babylon comes to prominence again in the time of Antichrist. It will of course be built up and modernised to become an important commercial centre. This can be deduced by the description of its wealth and trading when John is told of its final destruction in Revelation chapter 18.

There is no reason to believe that the Babylon of the book of Revelation is any other city. Only unbelief. We must remember not to fall into the trap of trying to fit current geopolitical countries and situations into prophecy. God's word will be fulfilled whether we are able to understand it now or not. *"With God all things are possible."* (Matthew 19:26 Luke 1:37)

One might ask, 'From which country will the Antichrist arise?'

Chapters thirty-eight and thirty-nine, of Ezekiel, give a strong indication. These two chapters make mention of several places, e.g. Magog, Meshech, Tubal, Gomer and Beth Togarmah. References to maps of the ancient Near East, or to gazetteers, indicate that these places are situated in what is modern day Turkey and its Black Sea neighbours. It would appear, therefore, that the rise of the Antichrist, and indeed, the seat of his power, will be in this region. (It is also true that these chapters, Ezekiel thirty-eight and thirty-nine, may, in part, be referring to the final rebellion at the end of the 1,000 year reign of Christ on earth. See Revelation 20:7-9)

Here, Ezekiel's prophecy seems to run hand in hand with that of Isaiah against the Assyrian (Isaiah 10:5-34 and 14:24-27). It is apparent that what Isaiah says goes much further than Sennacherib. The term 'Assyrian' referred to here, is more applicable to the Antichrist.

It is wrong to infer that Ezekiel 38 and 39 is a separate war campaign waged by Russia, as there are no convincing parallel scriptures to support this view (just as there is no scriptural support to the idea that the United Sates of America specifically features in Biblical prophecy, as some assert).

The idea of an invasion by Russia was especially popularised during the cold war era, when Russia seemed to be a military threat to the rest of the world. Zealous and over-anxious students of prophecy wrongly sought to fit the then current communist threat into biblical prophecy for the last days. Several Christian writers were particularly keen to do this in the seventies and, unfortunately, many Christians unquestioningly followed their lead. This idea has been preached by them for so long now that they seem unwilling to let go of it and admit they were wrong.

If Ezekiel 38 and 39 do refer to the time of Antichrist as well as to the final rebellion (Revelation 20:7-9), then besides the ten nation confederacy over which the Antichrist becomes the head (Revelation 17:12-14), there are many other nations that ally themselves with him. These include Persia (present day Iran and Iraq), Cush (present day Sudan) and Put (present day Libya) (Ezekiel 38:5).

Note that the countries mentioned are predominantly Muslim. If all the Christians are taken out of the world at the Rapture, it is almost certain that Islam will suddenly become the largest religion in the world.[2] I do not say that Islam will be the religion associated with the Antichrist (though that may be the case), but with the rise in Islamic fanaticism and Muslim's who openly vent their aggression and anger against the west, Christians and in particular, the Jews and Israel, to the extent that they are willing to blow themselves up to destroy the lives of others, it is not difficult to understand the fanaticism that will be associated with the worship of the Antichrist and Satan.

His followers will easily be persuaded to persecute to death both the Jews[3] and those people who become Christians after the Rapture. We only have to look at Kosovo and Slobodan Milosevic in 1999 to see that fanatical religious and ethnic cleansing can happen at anytime anywhere.[4]

It is certain that there will be a one-world religion of some sorts, for we read that:

> *"Men worshipped the dragon* [Satan] *because he had given authority to the beast, and they also worshipped the beast ... All the inhabitants of the earth will worship the beast ..."*
>
> Revelation 13:4 & 8

This will probably be similar to the emperor worship during the time of the Roman Empire. Certainly, the refusal of Christians to worship the Roman Emperors as "Lord" brought about terrible persecution of Christians - until, that is, Emperor

Constantine the Great embraced Christianity in AD 313, though it is highly unlikely that he ever was a true Christian. The "Marriage" of the Church and State was a marriage of convenience - for the convenience of the Roman Empire, that is!

The whole world will follow after the Antichrist. His reign will start off peaceably as if he were an apparent messiah with all the answers to the worlds problems, but will soon change into a brutal, satanic dictatorship with enforced compliance to his will.

The Antichrist will invade many countries (probably because they don't throw their lot in with him) and, as we have seen, set himself up in the Temple in Jerusalem[5] claiming to be God.[6] Military threats from the west, north and east will alarm him and he will lose heart.[7] In one last final campaign, he will gather his troops to the land of Israel, to Armageddon. This is what we read:

> *"Then they* [spirits of demons] *gathered the kings together to the place that in Hebrew is called Armageddon."*
>
> Revelation 16:16

> *"Then I saw the beast and the kings of the earth and their armies gathered together to make war against the Rider* [Christ] *on the horse and His army."*
>
> Revelation 19:19

> *"They will make war against the Lamb* [Christ]*, but the Lamb will overcome them because He is Lord of lords and King of kings..."*
>
> Revelation 17:14

"He [Antichrist] *will pitch his royal tents between the seas at the beautiful holy mountain. Yet he will come to his end, and no-one will help him."*

Daniel 11:45

"Then the Lord will go out and fight against those nations, as he fights in the day of battle."

Zechariah 14:3

"Out of His [Christ's] *mouth comes a sharp sword with which to strike down the nations. ... He treads the winepress of the fury of the wrath of God Almighty."*

Revelation 19:15

God will pour out His wrath and judgement upon the Antichrist, and the nations of the world gathered with him (Zephaniah 1:14-18 & 3:8), as he seeks to war against Christ when He returns to earth.

When Jesus does return to set up His earthly Kingdom, the Antichrist (the Beast) and the false prophet will be thrown alive into the Lake of Fire (Revelation 19:20). Satan will then be bound with a great chain and cast into the bottomless pit, out of harms way, for one thousand years (Revelation 20:1-3) (See also Ezekiel 38:18-39:8 / Zechariah 14:1-15).

Footnotes:

[1] Another instance when a statement made in scripture should be rightly divided in mid sentence for the correct interpretation is Isaiah 61:1-2. When the Lord Jesus quotes from this scripture, in Luke 4:17-20, He stops at the words, 'to proclaim the year of the Lord's favour'. If we look at Isaiah 61:2, where those words are written, we see that they continue with, 'and the day of vengeance of our God'. The former has been, and is being proclaimed, and was started by the Lord and His Apostles. The latter, as we know from history, has still not been fulfilled, which is why the Lord stopped short of quoting them. But they will be fulfilled, we believe, in the not too distant future.

[2] In 2000, estimated at well over one billion and growing fast.

[3] Anti Semitism is on the increase worldwide!

[4] Let's not forget it was Serb (so called) Christians that were killing Albanian Muslims in Kosovo! More recently, there has been more persecution of Christians in African countries (especially Sudan), Pakistan and Indonesia.

[5] The Temple must be built again. According to the *Jerusalem Post*, when a poll was taken in Israel in July 2002, at least 50% of those questioned wanted the Temple rebuilt.

[6] Revelation chapter 13 / Daniel 11:21-45 / Matthew 24:15 / 2 Thessalonians 2:4.

[7] Ezekiel 38:13 / Daniel 11:30 & 44 / Revelation 16:12-14.

WHAT ON EARTH IS GOING TO HAPPEN?

The sun will be turned to darkness and the moon to blood before the coming of the great and dreadful day of the Lord.

Joel 2:31

The sun turned black like sackcloth made of goat hair, the whole moon turned blood red.

Revelation 6:12

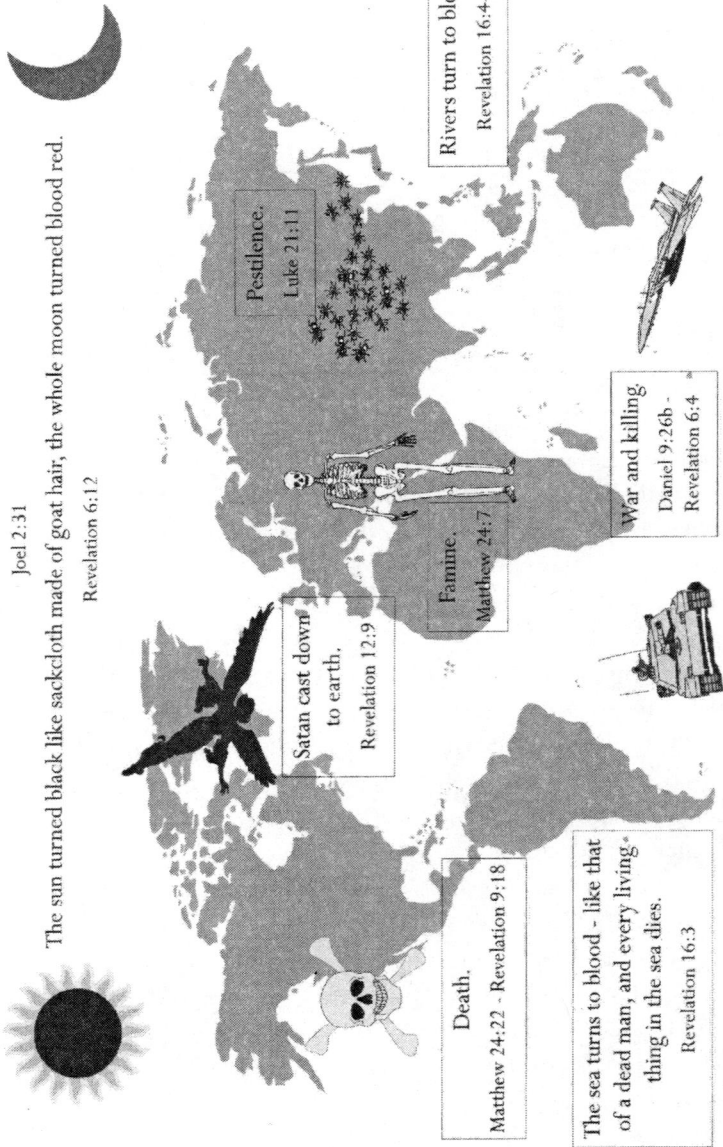

Rivers turn to blood.
Revelation 16:4-7

Pestilence.
Luke 21:11

War and killing.
Daniel 9:26b -
Revelation 6:4

Famine.
Matthew 24:7

Satan cast down
to earth.
Revelation 12:9

Death.
Matthew 24:22 - Revelation 9:18

The sea turns to blood - like that of a dead man, and every living thing in the sea dies.
Revelation 16:3

8

What on Earth is Going to Happen?

Jesus' disciples once asked Him a question:

"Tell us, .. when will this happen [the destruction of the temple at Jerusalem], *and what will be the sign of Your coming and of the end of the age?"*

Matthew 24:3

The Lord did not answer the first question, for God never gives dates in prophecy, but we know from history that the temple at Jerusalem was destroyed in AD 70. The answer to the second and third questions takes up most of the 24th and 25th chapters of Matthew's gospel (see also Luke chapter 21). It gave His disciples an insight into the things that would occur on the earth at the end of this age.

"You will hear of wars and rumours of wars, but see to it that you are not alarmed. Such things must happen, but the end is still to come. Nation will rise against nation, and kingdom against kingdom. There will be famines and earthquakes in various places."

Matthew 24:7

"There will be signs in the sun, moon and·stars. On the earth, nations will be in anguish and perplexity at the roaring and tossing of the sea. Men will faint from terror, apprehensive of

what is coming on the world, for the heavenly bodies will be shaken."

Luke 21:25-26

It is unlikely that the disciples could, in their day, have grasped fully the complexities of the things about which the Lord spoke as we can now in our lifetime. With the threat of nuclear, biological and chemical warfare techniques being employed by a growing number of nations in the world, it is understandable that people are in anguish and perplexed. It is also frightening to think that, because of the size of so many cities around the world in our day, an earthquake can wipe out tens of thousands of people in just a few moments.

Such horrors where tragically demonstrated in the earthquake off the coast of Indonesia on 26th December 2004. We saw so many countries and islands affected over such a wide area because of the resulting tsunami, which reached even to the east coast of Africa. Sadly, it is estimated that, altogether, 280,000 - 300,000 people lost there lives.

See what the Lord says:

*"There will be **great earthquakes**, famines and pestilences in various places, and **fearful events** and great signs from heaven."* (Emphasis added)

Luke 21:11

Note that it also says in that verse, *"**great signs from heaven**"*. With the technology we have now, it is simply amazing what tremendous events are being seen and understood in outer space. We are also witnessing catastrophic changes to our own atmosphere. Holes in the ozone layer, global warming, not to mention global dimming! We can only wonder at what might happen next.

We read, in the book of Revelation particularly, about specific events and details of things that are going to happen on the earth that go way past what we might imagine, or expect to happen, in the natural course of events. In many places it is like reading about the plagues of Egypt. God tells us about these terrible judgements not to frighten us, but to warn us that they will surely come.

Here is a list (not in order) of some of the things God tells us will happen:

- Peace is taken from the earth - Revelation 6:4.

- There will be war and desolations - Daniel 9:26b.

- The sun will turn black and the moon blood red; the stars will fall to earth and every mountain and island will be moved from its place - Revelation 6:12-14 / Joel 2:30-31.

- The earth will be 'broken up', 'split asunder' and 'thoroughly shaken' - Isaiah 13:9-13 & 24:17-20.

- A third of the earth and trees and all the grass will be burned up - Joel 1:15-20 / Revelation 8:7.

- Satan and his angels are cast out of Heaven and down to earth - Revelation 12:7-17.

- First a third, then all of the sea will turn to blood - Revelation 8:8 &16:3.

- A third of the rivers and springs of water will turn poisonous - then to blood - Revelation 8:10-11 & 16:4.

- There will be drought and plague - Revelation 11:6.

- A third of the sun, moon, stars, day and night will be struck with darkness - Revelation 8:12.

- The sun will scorch people with fire and they will be seared by intense heat - Revelation 16:8-9.

- Locusts with stings like scorpions will torment people for five months - Revelation 9:1-10.

- A third of mankind will be killed by what appears to be some kind of demonic army led by four angels - Revelation 9:13-19 / Joel 2:1-11

- The kingdom of the Antichrist will be plunged into darkness - Revelation 16:10.

- The great city of Babylon will be completely destroyed - Revelation 18:1-24.

- Hailstones weighing about a hundred pounds each will fall on men - Revelation 16:21.

As we can see, after the Church has been resurrected and raptured away to heaven, the earth is not going to be a pleasant place when these judgements are poured out. It is the time when God will no longer put up with the evil and wickedness in the world but will send His Son Jesus Christ to reign over the earth forever and ever.

> *"The nations were angry; and Your wrath has come. The time has come for judging the dead, and for rewarding Your servants the prophets and Your saints and those who reverence Your name, both small and great - and for destroying those who destroy the earth."*
>
> Revelation 11:18

God, in His grace and love towards mankind, is currently giving the world time to repent and to trust in His Son Jesus Christ for Salvation. He promises to remove His Church from the world before He judges it, as we have already seen.

> *"... Jesus, who rescues us from the coming wrath."*

> *"For God did not appoint us to suffer wrath but to receive salvation through our Lord Jesus Christ."*
>
> 1 Thessalonians 1:10 & 5:9

> *"Since we have now been justified by His blood, how much more shall we be saved from God's wrath through Him!"*
>
> Romans 5:9

In the Bible we are encouraged by God both to read and take to heart what He has promised He is going to do on the earth:

> *"Blessed is the one who reads the words of this prophecy, and*

blessed are those who take to heart what is written in it, because the time is near."

Revelation 1:3

"The angel said to me, 'these words are trustworthy and true. The Lord, the God of the spirits of the prophets, sent His angel to show His servants the things that must soon take place.' 'Behold, I am coming soon! Blessed is he who keeps the words of this prophecy in this book.'"

Revelation 22:6-7

"Then he told me, 'Do not seal up the words of the prophecy of this book, because the time is near.'"

"I, Jesus, have sent My angel to give you this testimony for the churches. ..."

Revelation 22:10 and 16

Those who will believe in the true and living God who created the world and everything in it and who come to Jesus Christ, the only Saviour, for forgiveness of sins and eternal life, are exhorted to believe also in the prophecies concerning the end times. God has spoken about them for good reason. Those who take heed of them can be prepared and keep trusting that God is working everything out according to His predetermined plan for getting rid of all evil and wickedness from the world and setting up His righteous kingdom, where Jesus Christ will truly be the *"King of kings and Lord of lords"* (Revelation 19:16).

The world ignores these warnings at its peril.

9

Those Who Become Christians
after the Rapture

Some are concerned that, after the Church has been resurrected and Raptured to be with the Lord in heaven, it will then be too late to get right with God and for sinners to come to the Lord Jesus Christ for salvation. But scripture shows that this concern is unfounded. It is evident that after the Church has been taken up to Heaven, there will be multitudes of people who put their faith and trust in Jesus and become Christians.

*"After this I looked and there before me was **a great multitude that no one could count**, from every nation, tribe, people and language, standing before the throne and in front of the Lamb. They were wearing white robes and were holding palm branches in their hands. And they cried out in a loud voice: 'Salvation belongs to our God, who sits on the throne, and to the Lamb.' ... 'These are **they who have come out of the great tribulation**; they have washed their robes and made them white in the blood of the Lamb.'"* (Emphasis added)

Revelation 7:9-10 & 14

"The Spirit and the bride say, 'Come!' And let him who hears say, 'Come!' Whoever is thirsty, let him come; and whoever wishes, let him take the free gift of the water of life."

Revelation 22:17

It is these Christians who will be here when the Antichrist rules and when the judgements of God are poured out on the earth. Many Christians today get these two groups, the Church and the Tribulation Christians, confused, and wrongfully apply scriptures to the Church that are meant for the Tribulation Christians and vice versa. This has led many Christians to believe that the Church is going to go through the Tribulation, which, as we have seen previously, is not what God teaches in His word.

There will be *"another beast"*, referred to elsewhere as *"the false prophet"* (Rev. 13:11 & 19:20), who will exercise all the authority of the Antichrist. He will *"perform great and miraculous signs"* (Rev. 13:13) and cause restrictions on people's ability to buy and sell.

> *"He also forced everyone, small and great, rich and poor, free and slave, to receive a mark on his right hand or forehead, so that no one could buy or sell unless he had the mark, which is the name of the beast or the number of his name. ... His number is 666."*
>
> Revelation 13:16-18

This means that those who do not worship the beast and do not take this 'mark' will become outcasts from society and will be persecuted to death.

> *"He was given power to give breath to the image of the first beast, so that it could speak and cause all who refused to worship the image to be killed."*
>
> Revelation 13:15

"Then the dragon was enraged at the woman and went off to make war against the rest of her offspring - those who obey God's commandments and hold to the testimony of Jesus."

Revelation 12:17

The Tribulation Christians will not allow themselves to have the mark of the Beast, either on their hand or forehead. They will be prepared to take the consequences of disobeying the Antichrist and the false prophet because they will know that to give in to them will bring upon themselves condemnation from God.

"A third angel followed them and said in a loud voice: 'If anyone worships the beast [Antichrist] *and his image and receives his mark on the forehead or on the hand, he, too, will drink the wine of God's fury, which has been poured full strength into the cup of His wrath. He will be tormented with burning sulphur in the presence of the holy angels and of the Lamb. And the smoke of their torment rises forever and ever. There is no rest day or night for those who worship the beast and his image, or for anyone who receives the mark of his name.'"*

Revelation 14:9-11

We also read that during this time:

"If anyone is to go into captivity, into captivity he will go. If anyone is to be killed with the sword, with the sword he will be killed. This calls for patient endurance and faithfulness on the part of the saints."

Revelation 13:10

"This calls for patient endurance on the part of the saints who obey God's commandments and remain faithful to Jesus."

Revelation 14:12

It is evident, from what is said, that these believers will suffer because of the plagues that are poured out on the earth, even though they are not the ones targeted for these judgements. However, the Christians who live during this time will be rewarded for their faith and endurance:

"Never again will they hunger; never again will they thirst. The sun will not beat upon them, nor any scorching heat. ... And God will wipe away every tear from their eyes."

Revelation 7:16-17

During the time of God's wrath and judgement upon the earth, He will still seek to win souls to His Son Jesus Christ so that they may be saved. He will do this by sending an angel to proclaim, from the air, the Eternal Gospel. The angel will exhort the inhabitants of the earth to fear God and give Him the glory.

"Then I saw another angel flying in mid-air, and he had the eternal gospel to proclaim to those who live on earth - to every nation, tribe, language and people. He said in a loud voice, 'Fear God and give Him glory, because the hour of His judgment has come. Worship Him who made the heavens, the earth, the sea and the springs of water.'"

Revelation 14:6-7

"And everyone who calls on the name of the Lord will be saved."
Joel 2:32

Those who are believers will, no doubt, be spreading the good news of Jesus Christ as much as they can. Those who are killed for their faith in Christ are seen briefly under the altar in heaven, asking the Lord how long they have to wait before their blood is avenged. They are told that they have to wait until the number of their fellow servants who are to be killed, as they were, is completed (Revelation 6:9-11). Later, when the Lord returns to earth, they will be resurrected from the dead and reign with Christ for one thousand years (Revelation 20:4).

Many believe that, along with the Tribulation saints, God will resurrect the Old Testament saints, as it is obvious that they are not part of the Church. It is suggested that they, along with the tribulation saints who are killed, are the guests spoken about in the parable of the wedding banquet in Matthew 22:1-14. Christ Jesus, of course, is the Bridegroom, and the Church, the Bride.

Millions of people will die in the wars and devastation of the earth during this time of God's judgement. God tells us:

"I will make man scarcer than pure gold, more rare than the gold of Ophir." ... "Therefore a curse consumes the earth; its people must bear their guilt. Therefore earth's inhabitants are burned up, and very few are left."
Isaiah 13:12 & 24:6

Though there will be few inhabitants left, there will still be Christians and unbelievers living when the Lord returns to the earth. The Christians will know that there is an end to

God's judgements and will be waiting for Him to appear.

When the Lord returns to the earth to set up His Kingdom, all the people that are left alive of the nations of the earth will be gathered before Him and He will then divide everyone into two groups:

"When the Son of Man [Jesus] comes in His glory, and all the angels with Him, He will sit on His throne in heavenly glory. All the nations will be gathered before Him, and He will separate the people one from another as a shepherd separates the sheep from the goats ."

Matthew 25:31-32

The saved will be welcomed into His Kingdom. Each, by giving the other food, drink and clothing, as they had need, will have supported their fellow believers through those terrible days.

"Then the King will say to those on His right, 'Come, you who are blessed by My Father; take your inheritance, the Kingdom prepared for you since the creation of the world. ... I tell you the truth, whatever you did for one of the least of these brothers of Mine, you did for Me.'"

Matthew 25:34-40

The unsaved, having done none of these things, will be condemned and go away into eternal punishment.

"Then He will say to those on His left, 'Depart from Me, you who are cursed, into the eternal fire prepared for the devil and his angels. ...' 'Then they will go away to eternal punishment,

but the righteous to eternal life.'"

Matthew 25:41-46

When the Lord comes back from Heaven to earth, all the Christians who make up the Church and were resurrected and raptured before the judgement of God fell, will return with Him.

"... See, the Lord is coming with thousands upon thousands of His holy ones. ..."

Jude 14

"The armies of heaven were following Him, riding on white horses and dressed in fine linen, white and clean."

Revelation 19:14
(See also Zechariah 14:5b)

Everyone the world over will see Jesus returning from heaven to earth and know that He is the Son of God, King of kings and Lord of lords. Nationally, Israel will finally acknowledge that Jesus of Nazareth, the One whom they crucified some two thousand years or so before, really is their long awaited Messiah.

"Look, He is coming with the clouds, and every eye will see Him, even those [Israel] who pierced Him; and all the peoples of the earth will mourn because of Him. So shall it be! Amen."

Revelation 1:7
(See also Isaiah 52:8-10)

"And I will pour out on the house of David and the inhabitants

of Jerusalem a spirit of grace and supplication. They will look on Me, the one they have pierced, [Jesus] and they will mourn for Him as one mourns for an only child, and grieve bitterly for Him as one grieves for a firstborn son."

Zechariah 12:10

Then those who are left of the nation of Israel will fulfil the words spoken by the Lord Jesus just a few days before they shouted for His crucifixion:

"For I tell you, you will not see Me again until you say, 'Blessed is He who comes in the name of the Lord.'"

Matthew 23:39

10

Israel

The apostle Paul wrote the following:

"I do not want you to be ignorant of this mystery, ... Israel has experienced a hardening in part until the full number of the Gentiles has come in. **And so all Israel will be saved**, *... as far as the election is concerned, they are loved on account of the patriarchs, for God's gifts and His call are irrevocable."* (Emphasis added)

Romans 11:25-29

All through the writings of the Old Testament prophets, we see how the people of Israel turned away from the Lord and sinned against Him, causing His judgement to come upon them. Though the Lord sent them many prophets to warn them and turn them back to Himself, they would not listen. Finally, God sent His only Son, the Messiah Jesus, with the hope that the people of Israel would listen to Him, but instead, they crucified Him. Three days later, however, God raised Jesus from the dead and He is alive now for evermore. We might have expected that God would have done with Israel.[1] But He didn't. Within a few weeks, the Lord had sent His messenger to the people of Israel to tell them that if they would repent, their sins would be forgiven and they would receive the gift of the Holy Spirit. Thousands of Jews accepted the message then (Acts 2:38-42), and many in our day know Messiah Jesus as their

Saviour. But sadly, Israel as a whole, even to this day, has rejected Jesus who could save them from all their troubles.

As a Jew and descendant of king David, Jesus the Messiah is the rightful King of Israel, but the scripture has yet to be fulfilled that says,

> *"The Lord will be King over the whole earth."*
>
> Zechariah 14:9

God's plan is slowly being worked out in accordance with His time and will. We are witnessing, in our days, the fulfilment of prophecy with regard to God re-gathering the Jews back to the land of Israel.

> *"I myself will gather the remnant of my flock out of all the countries where I have driven them and will bring them back to their pasture, where they will be fruitful and increase in number."*
>
> Jeremiah 23:3

> *"For I will take you out of the nations; I will gather you from all the countries and bring you back into your own land."*
>
> Ezekiel 36:24
>
> (See also: Isaiah 43:1-7 / Ezekiel 37:21 / Amos 9:14-15)

As a nation they are back in the land of Israel (albeit in unbelief), but God will take them through the refining fires during the Great Tribulation until they acknowledge Jesus as their Messiah King and know that He is the Lord their God.

> *"'In the whole land,' declares the Lord, 'two-thirds will be*

struck down and perish; yet one-third will be left in it. This third I will bring into the fire; I will refine them like silver and test them like gold. They will call on My name and I will answer them; I will say, 'They are My people,' and they will say, 'the Lord is our God.'"

Zechariah 13:8-9

(See also: Jeremiah 30:1-11 / Ezekiel 39:25-29)

Israel will make some sort of seven year alliance with the Antichrist (Daniel 9:27), and this is what seems to be their undoing. Jesus referred to this when He said,

"I have come in My Fathers name, and you do not accept Me; but if someone else comes in his own name, you will accept him."

John 5:43

The Antichrist will break the covenant with Israel after three and a half years, and set himself up in the rebuilt temple of God in Jerusalem, proclaiming to be God.

"He [Antichrist] will confirm a covenant with many [in Israel] for one 'seven' [seven years]. In the middle of the 'seven' he will put an end to sacrifice and offering. And on a wing of the temple he will set up an abomination that causes desolation, until the end that is decreed is poured out on him."

Daniel 9:27

"He [Antichrist] will oppose and will exalt himself over everything that is called God or is worshipped, so that he sets himself up in God's temple, proclaiming himself to be God"

2 Thessalonians 2:4

This will be the beginning of the Great Tribulation period. We know that, down through history, the Jews have always been persecuted. There have been many pogroms against them, but no persecution so brutal and horrific as the Nazi persecution during the Second World War. The death camps set up for the mass murder of men, women and children leave one cold and speechless at man's inhumanity to man. How could the world ever forget the Holocaust? And yet the same thing is going to happen in the future. Satan, for that is who is behind such persecution, will again pursue and seek to destroy the Jews. However, God tells us that this time He will intervene in a very special and miraculous way. He will give His chosen people help and assistance in the form of a place prepared in the desert for them, to which they will flee and be looked after for three and a half years.

"The woman [Israel] fled into the desert to a place prepared for her by God, where she might be taken care of for 1,260 days ... When the dragon [Satan] saw that he had been hurled to earth, he pursued the woman [Israel] who had given birth to the male child [Jesus]. The woman was given the wings of a great eagle, so that she might fly to the place prepared for her in the desert, where she could be taken care of for a time, times and half a time [3½ years], out of the serpent's reach. ... Then the dragon was enraged at the woman and went off to make war against the rest of her offspring - those who obey God's commandments and hold to the testimony of Jesus."

Revelation 12:6 & 13-14 & 17

This desert place could well be in the country of Jordan (Ancient Edom, Moab and Ammon), which will be delivered from the armies of the Antichrist in their invasion of the Middle East.

> *"He will also invade the Beautiful Land. Many countries will fall, but Edom, Moab and the leaders of Ammon will be delivered from his hand."*
>
> Daniel 11:41

It has been suggested by some that the place where the Jewish people will seek refuge at this time of persecution is the ancient city of Petra, which is situated in south-western Jordan. Petra, which had fallen into ruin over the centuries, was discovered by Johann Burckhardt in 1812. Apparently, to reach the city one has to travel through a narrow ravine, which at times is only a few metres wide - an ideal place to defend against any who would attack. But this is, of course, just speculation.

During this time, God will have 144,000 servants from all the tribes of Israel and it appears that they will be God's chosen witnesses to Israel and the nations.

> *"'Do not harm the land or the sea or the trees until we put a seal on the foreheads of the servants of our God.' Then I heard the number of those who were sealed: 144,000 from all the tribes of Israel."*
>
> Revelation 7:3-4
>
> (See also Revelation 14:1-5 / Isaiah 43:10-13)

There will also be two special witnesses during this time, who will prophesy and be given miraculous powers by God. It is most likely that the time of their prophetic witness will be the first half of the seven year period (Daniel's seventieth week) referred to earlier. No one will be able to hurt them during their time of ministry and they will be able to do astounding miraculous things:

> *"These men have power to shut up the sky so that it will not rain during the time they are prophesying; and they have power to turn the waters into blood and to strike the earth with every kind of plague as often as they want."*
>
> Revelation 11:6

After three and a half years their prophetic ministry will come to an end and these two witnesses will be killed in Jerusalem. Their dead bodies, having been left in the street for all to see, will, after three and a half days, be resurrected and taken up to heaven in full view of everyone. At that very hour there will be a severe earthquake in Jerusalem, resulting in the death of 7,000 people (Revelation 11:7-14). The seven bowls of God's wrath will then be poured out on the world (Revelation 16:1-21), culminating, as we indicated earlier, in the physical return to earth of the Lord Jesus Christ with the armies of heaven (Revelation 19:11-21). Then the nation of Israel will finally acknowledge that Jesus is their Messiah, and the Lord will make a new covenant with them, forgive their wickedness and remember their sins no more.

> *"And I will pour out on the house of David and the inhabitants of Jerusalem a spirit of grace and supplication. They will look on Me* [Jesus] *the one they have pierced, and they will mourn for Him as one mourns for an only child, and grieve bitterly for Him as one grieves for a firstborn son."*
>
> Zechariah 12:10

"'The time is coming,' declares the Lord, 'when I will make a new covenant with the house of Israel and with the house of Judah. It will not be like the covenant I made with their forefathers when I took them by the hand to lead them out of Egypt, because they broke my covenant, ... This is the covenant that I will make with the house of Israel after that time,' declares the Lord. 'I will put My law in their minds and write it on their hearts. I will be their God, and they will be My people. ... 'For I will forgive their wickedness and will remember their sins no more.'"

Jeremiah 31:31-34

After the Lord Jesus has judged the nations (Matthew 25:31-46), He will set up His earthly Kingdom and reign in righteousness, from Jerusalem, over the whole earth.

"The Lord will be King over the whole earth. On that day there will be one Lord, and His name the only name."

Zechariah 14:9

"Why do the nations conspire and the peoples plot in vain? The kings of the earth take their stand and the rulers gather together against the LORD and against His Anointed One. 'Let us break their chains,' they say, 'and throw off their fetters.'

"The One enthroned in heaven laughs; the Lord scoffs at them. Then He rebukes them in His anger and terrifies them in His wrath, saying, 'I have installed My King on Zion, My holy hill. "I will proclaim the decree of the LORD: He said to Me, 'You are My Son; today I have become Your Father. Ask of Me, and I will make the nations Your inheritance, the ends of the

earth Your possession. You will rule them with an iron scepter;
You will dash them to pieces like pottery.'"

Psalm 2:1-9

Footnotes

---

[1] There is an idea held by some known as 'Replacement Theology'. Simply put, the idea is that God has rejected Israel and replaced it with the Church. In light of scripture it seems to me to be difficult to understand how this 'false' doctrine ever came about. The Apostle Paul writes in Romans:

"I ask then: Did God reject his people? **By no means!** *I am an Israelite myself, a descendant of Abraham, from the tribe of Benjamin.* **God did not reject his people,** *whom he foreknew."* (Emphasis added) Romans 11:1-2a.

A closer read of Romans chapter 9 verse 30 through to chapter 11 verse 32 explains a great deal about God's present dealings with Israel and why. There is no doubt that God puts a difference between the nation of Israel and the Gentile nations. Only in His Church, the body of Christ, are Jew and Gentile brought together and made one (see Ephesians 2:11-22). In the Millennial reign of Christ it is evident that distinction continues to be made between the Nation of Israel and the Gentile nations. Israel is very much alive and well as can be seen by the land allocated to the Twelve Tribes as noted in Ezekiel 47 & 48. Here we are told what area Israel will cover. Simply put, the north border will be, roughly, from present day Tripoli in Lebanon east to roughly 30 miles inland. From there the eastern border will go south to pick up the Jordan River and continue through Lake Galilee and the Dead Sea. The southern border will be from the southern tip of the Dead Sea bearing southwest until it picks up a brook that flows from Sinai (*"Meribah Kadesh"*). From there it follows the brook to the Mediterranean near a place called El Arish in Egypt. From there the western boundary will be northward, along the coast of the Mediterranean, back to Tripoli where we started. So we can see that the 'Replacement Theology' doctrine is completely false.

THE MILLENNIAL REIGN OF CHRIST

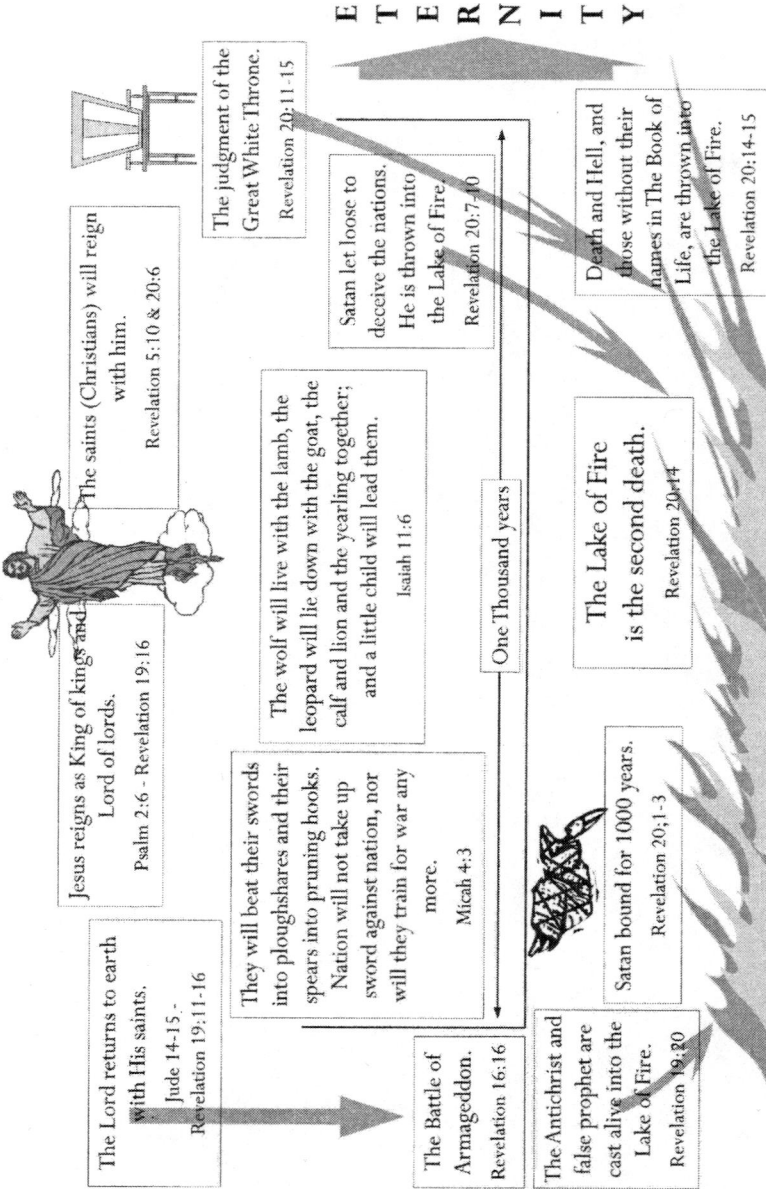

E
T
E
R
N
I
T
Y

The judgment of the Great White Throne.
Revelation 20:11-15

Jesus reigns as King of kings and Lord of lords.
Psalm 2:6 - Revelation 19:16

The saints (Christians) will reign with him.
Revelation 5:10 & 20:6

Satan let loose to deceive the nations. He is thrown into the Lake of Fire.
Revelation 20:7-10

Death and Hell, and those without their names in The Book of Life, are thrown into the Lake of Fire.
Revelation 20:14-15

The wolf will live with the lamb, the leopard will lie down with the goat, the calf and lion and the yearling together; and a little child will lead them.
Isaiah 11:6

They will beat their swords into ploughshares and their spears into pruning hooks. Nation will not take up sword against nation, nor will they train for war any more.
Micah 4:3

One Thousand years

The Lake of Fire is the second death.
Revelation 20:14

The Lord returns to earth with His saints.
Jude 14-15 - Revelation 19:11-16

The Battle of Armageddon.
Revelation 16:16

The Antichrist and false prophet are cast alive into the Lake of Fire.
Revelation 19:20

Satan bound for 1000 years.
Revelation 20;1-3

11

The Millennial Reign of Christ

The thousand year reign, on earth, of the Lord Jesus Christ, will be a time of great blessing, for Israel and all the nations of the world alike. Revelation chapter 19:11-21 describes the conclusion of the dreadful events that will occur at the time of the Lord's return. He will return to earth accompanied by the armies of heaven. War will ensue with, on the one hand, the beast, earth's kings and their armies, and, on the other, the Word of God (Jesus) and the heavenly armies. The destruction will be like none other in the entire history of mankind.

> *"How awful that day will be! None will be like it. It will be a time of trouble for Jacob* [Israel], *but he will be saved out of it."*
>
> Jeremiah 30:7

> *"For then there will be great distress, unequalled from the beginning of the world until now - and never to be equalled again. If those days had not been cut short, no-one would survive, but for the sake of the elect those days will be shortened."*
>
> Matthew 24:21-22

Though we cannot be sure, it would appear, from the language employed, that the events will include nuclear exchanges.

> *"This is the plague with which the Lord will strike all the nations that fought against Jerusalem: Their flesh will rot while they are still standing on their feet, their eyes will rot in their sockets, and their tongues will rot in their mouths. ... A similar plague will strike the horses and mules, the camels and donkeys, and all the animals in those camps."*
>
> Zechariah 14:12&15

> *"'Surely the day is coming; it will burn like a furnace. All the arrogant and every evildoer will be stubble, and that day that is coming will set them on fire,' says the Lord Almighty. 'Not a root or a branch will be left to them.'"*
>
> Malachi 4:1

So great will be the numbers of the dead that the Lord will call upon wild animals, and birds of the air in helping with the disposal of the carnage.

> *"And I saw an angel standing in the sun, who cried in a loud voice to all the birds flying in mid air, 'Come, gather together for the great supper of God, so that you may eat the flesh of kings, generals, and mighty men, of horses and their riders, and the flesh of all people, free and slave, small and great.'"*
>
> Revelation 19:17-18
> (See also Ezekiel 39:17-20)

Incredibly, it appears that crude and basic wooden hand weapons will have been used in this battle, besides modern weapons of mass destruction. These weapons, we are told, will be used for fuel for seven years, and there will be so many dead that it will take seven months for Israel to bury the bodies.

> *"Then those who live in the towns of Israel will go out and use the weapons for fuel and burn them up - the small and the large shields, the bows and arrows, the war clubs and spears. For seven years they will use them for fuel."*
>
> Ezekiel 39:9

> *"For seven months the house of Israel will be burying them* [Gog and his hordes] *in order to cleanse the land."*
>
> Ezekiel 39:12

The Lord Jesus will reign in glory and will judge righteously and justly between the nations of the world. Then, at last, there will be true peace, of a kind which the world has not known since those wondrous days in the Garden of Eden, in His never ending government. All peoples will be taught by Him from Jerusalem, where they will go to worship Him.

> *"Many peoples will come and say, 'Come, let us go up to the mountain of the Lord, to the house of the God of Jacob* [Israel], *He will teach us His ways, so that we may walk in His paths.' The law will go out from Zion, the word of the Lord from Jerusalem. He will judge between the nations and will settle disputes for many peoples. They will beat their swords into ploughshares and their spears into pruning hooks. Nation will not take up sword against nation, nor will they train for war any more."*
>
> Isaiah 2:3-4

(See also Isaiah 9:7 / 32:1 / 62:1-12 / Zechariah 14:16)

When the Lord returns from Heaven, it is only those who are saved at the judgement of the nations that remain and enter Christ's Kingdom on earth (Matthew 25:31-46). During this one thousand year reign of Christ on earth, all of creation will be liberated from its bondage to decay, and dangerous creatures will become harmless.

"The creation waits in eager expectation for the sons of God to be revealed. For the creation was subject to frustration, not by its own choice, but by the will of the One Who subjected it, in hope that the creation itself will be liberated from its bondage to decay and brought into the glorious freedom of the children of God."

Romans 8:19-21

"The wolf will live with the lamb, the leopard will lie down with the goat, the calf and the lion and the yearling together, and a little child will lead them. The cow will feed with the bear, their young will lie down together, and the lion will eat straw like the ox. The infant will play near the hole of the cobra, and the young child put his hand into the viper's nest. They will neither harm nor destroy on all my holy mountain, for the earth will be full of the knowledge of the Lord as the waters cover the sea."

Isaiah 11:6-9

On earth, longevity will return (i.e. people will live for hundreds of years, as they did before the flood in Noah's day).

"Never again will there be in it an infant who lives but a few days, or an old man who does not live out his years; he who dies

at a hundred will be thought a mere youth; he who fails to reach a hundred will be considered accursed."

Isaiah 65:20

A new temple will be built at Jerusalem and sacrifices of animals will again be instituted (see Ezekiel chapter 40:1 through to 47:12).

The population of the earth will again increase until the earth is full of people, as the Lord originally intended when He first made man:

"God blessed them and said to them, 'Be fruitful and increase in number; fill the earth and subdue it. Rule over the fish of the sea and the birds of the air and over every living creature that moves on the ground.'"

Genesis 1:28

The resurrected and raptured now glorified Church will reign with Christ during His one thousand year reign. It may be in some supervisory or overseeing capacity, making sure the Lord's will is carried out on earth. Unlike those living on earth their role will be of a heavenly nature, for that is where they will belong for time and eternity.

It is said of Christians:

*"But our citizenship is **in heaven**. ..."* (Emphasis added)

Philippians 3:20

*"And into an inheritance that can never perish, spoil or fade - kept **in heaven** for you."* (Emphasis added)

1 Peter 1:4

The resurrected Tribulation Christians, those who are martyred for their faith during the Tribulation, will also reign with Christ for the one thousand years (Revelation 20:4).

Satan will be bound and locked up in the Abyss for the one thousand year reign of Christ on earth. During that time he will not be able to deceive anyone. At the end of the one thousand years he will be set free again, perhaps as a testing time for the nations to see if their hearts are truly at one with God. He will again be at his old tricks and will deceive many among the nations. He will stir up discontentment, anger and rebellion against God among many people and will cause them to gather together for battle against the Lord and against Jerusalem. But God will destroy them by fire from heaven, and the Devil will be cast into the Lake of Fire forever, never to deceive or destroy again.

> *"And I saw an angel coming down out of Heaven, having the key to the Abyss and holding in his hand a great chain. He seized the dragon, that ancient serpent, who is the Devil or Satan, and bound him for a thousand years. He threw him into the Abyss, and locked and sealed it over him, to keep him from deceiving the nations anymore until the thousand years were ended. After that, he must be set free for a short time."*
>
> Revelation 20:1-3

> *"When the thousand years are over, Satan will be released from his prison and will go out to deceive the nations in the four corners of the earth - Gog and Magog - to gather them for battle. In number they are like the sand on the seashore. They marched across the breadth of the earth and surrounded the camp of God's people, the city He loves [Jerusalem]. But fire*

came down from Heaven and devoured them. And the Devil,
who deceived them, was thrown into the lake of burning
sulphur, where the beast and the false prophet had been
thrown. They will be tormented day and night for ever and
ever."

Revelation 20:7-10

Then God will sit upon His great white throne and the
unsaved dead will be raised and judged according to what they
did during their lifetime on earth.

"Then I saw a great white throne and Him Who was seated
upon it. Earth and sky fled from His presence, and there was no
place for them. And I saw the dead, great and small, standing
before the throne, and books were opened. Another book was
opened, which is the book of life. The dead were judged
according to what they had done as recorded in the books. The
sea gave up the dead that were in it, and death and Hades gave
up the dead that were in them, and each person was judged
according to what he had done. Then death and Hades were
thrown into the Lake of Fire. The Lake of Fire is the second
death. If anyone's name was not found written in the book of
life, he was thrown into the Lake of Fire."

Revelation 20:11-15

There is no mention of the sacrificial death and
resurrection of the Lord Jesus Christ here; we can only
conclude, therefore, that none of those who are judged at the
Great White Throne will escape eternal punishment. They,
along with death and hell, will be thrown into the Lake of Fire.
This is referred to as the second death and is where the

Antichrist and the false prophet will have already been for one thousand years (Revelation 19:20), and where Satan also will be.

Notice that if anyone is not 'born again' according to the Lord Jesus' words in John's Gospel, chapter 3:3, then, because they have rejected God's offer of salvation through Jesus Christ, they will have to die twice! Once in physical death; then, after they have been resurrected to appear before the Great White Throne judgment, the second death, which is the Lake of Fire (Revelation 20:14). What a grave and sobering thought that is. I trust that you, the reader of these words, if not a Christian, will not put off salvation through faith in the Lord Jesus Christ any longer, but that you will put your trust and faith in Him now, while He calls you to repentance, so that you may have forgiveness of sins and eternal life through Him.

Finally:

"Then the end will come, when He [Christ] hands over the Kingdom to God the Father after He has destroyed all dominion, authority and power. For He must reign until He has put all His enemies under His feet. The last enemy to be destroyed is death. For He 'has put everything under His feet' [Psalm 8:6]. Now when it says that 'everything' has been put under Him, it is clear that this does not include God Himself, Who put everything under Christ. When He has done this, then the Son Himself will be made subject to Him Who put everything under Him, so that God may be all in all."

1 Corinthians 15:24-28

After this, God will destroy the present earth and heaven with fire and create a new heaven and new earth, where sin and wickedness will no longer dwell but where righteousness and peace will reside for ever. Indeed, a place where God will dwell with mankind throughout eternity.

> *"Then I saw a new heaven and a new earth, for the first heaven and the first earth had passed away, and there was no longer any sea."*
>
> Revelation 21:1

> *"Behold, I create new heavens and a new earth. The former things will not be remembered, nor will they come to mind."*
>
> Isaiah 65:17

> *"... That day will bring about the destruction of the heavens by fire, and the elements will melt in the heat. But in keeping with His promise we are looking forward to a new heaven and a new earth, the home of righteousness."*
>
> 2 Peter 3:12b-13

There appears to be very little in the scriptures about the saved of the nations who remain on the earth at the second coming of Christ, and who are welcomed into His one thousand year earthly Kingdom, apart, that is, from those that clearly state that they will be blessed by God. We are only given glimpses of what the Millennial reign of the Lord Jesus Christ will be like, but we can be sure that it will be wonderful and far exceed anything we could imagine (see Psalms 45, 46, 47 etc.). Also, little is mentioned about those who will be born and saved during it. But we can be sure that it will be a time of peace, growth and prosperity for all people; a time when all people will be able to live without fear of violence, aggression or provocation. Indeed, it will be as close to Utopia as one could get.

Apart from those who are deceived and who rebel against the Lord when, for a little while, at the end of the one thousand years, Satan is loosed from his chains and from the Abyss, it is almost certain that those who live during the time of the Millennium will be the ones who inhabit the new earth for eternity (see Revelation chapter 21).

Those who belong to the Lord and who have died during the time of the Millennium must be resurrected at the end, though there are no specific scriptures that speak of this. We can be assured that God will work out everything according to His will.

"And we know that in all things God works for the good of those who love Him, who have been called according to His purpose."

Romans 8:28

"Will not the Judge of all the earth do right?"

Genesis 18:25b

"I will proclaim the name of the LORD. Oh, praise the greatness of our God! He is the Rock, His works are perfect, and all His ways are just. A faithful God who does no wrong, upright and just is He."

Deuteronomy 32:3-4

ETERNITY

The Son hands over the Kingdom to the Father; the last enemy, death, is destroyed and God is All in All.
1 Corinthians 15:24-28

His servants will serve Him. They will see his face. They will reign for ever and ever.
Revelation 22:3-5

Full joy and eternal pleasures in God's presence for ever.
Psalm 16:11

The new heavens and new earth.
2 Peter 3:13 & Revelation 21:1

New Jerusalem coming down out of heaven from God.
Revelation 21:10-11

The present heavens and earth destroyed by fire.
2 Peter 3:7 & 12

For ever and ever ......

The Lake of Fire is The Second death
Revelation 20:14

There will be weeping and gnashing of teeth - where the worm does not die and the fire is not quenched.
Matthew 13:49-50 - Mark 9:48

Blackest darkness.
2 Peter 2:17 - Jude 13

The eternal place of Satan and his angels, and all the wicked dead

THE END OF TIME

12

Eternity

In this introductory study of the Return of Jesus Christ, we have reached the point where time ends and eternity begins. God, having redeemed multitudes through the sacrificial death and resurrection of the Lord Jesus Christ, will condemn the unregenerate, along with the Devil and his angels, to the lake of fire. Having done away with the old order of things, God will create a new heaven and earth. Sin and death will be no more:

> *"He will wipe every tear from there eyes. There will be no more death or mourning or crying or pain, for the old order of things has passed away. He who was seated on the throne said, 'I am making everything new!' Then He said, 'write this down, for these words are trustworthy and true'"*
>
> Revelation 21:4-5

and God will be all in all.

> *"When He has done this, then the Son Himself will be made subject to Him Who put everything under Him, so that God may be all in all."*
>
> 1 Corinthians 15:28

It is impossible for our human, finite minds to comprehend the concept of eternity. Doubtless, God never intended that we should discern such whilst we are here on earth. Our lives are very much governed by time, with some things even measured to the nearest one thousandth of a second. Each second or minute, each hour or day, each week, month or year has an end before the next starts. Eternity, however, never ends. It is immeasurable.

The Almighty, Holy, Righteous, and All Powerful God, whose amazing love and mercy toward us is so unfathomable, withholds nothing, in order to determine that mankind, whom He has created and who have sinned so wickedly against Him in time, can be rescued from the consequences and power of our sin. We can be changed, made ready to enter eternity, holy and righteous - in a state of sinless perfection - so that we may have unhindered union and eternal fellowship with Him!

> *"And I heard a loud voice from the throne saying, 'Now the dwelling of God is with men, and He will live with them. They will be His people, and God Himself will be with them and be their God.'"*

Revelation 21:3
(See also John 17: 20-24)

In his visions on the Isle of Patmos, the apostle John had a tiny glimpse into eternity. He saw the new heavens and the new earth, in which there will be no more death, or mourning, or crying, or pain. The Church is referred to as Christ's *"Bride"* (Revelation 19:7). John saw the Holy City, New Jerusalem, coming down out of Heaven from God, and the angel referred to it as *"the bride, the wife of the Lamb"* (Revelation 21:9). It is feasible that this is the eternal home - the many rooms of the Fathers house (John 14:2) - of those of the redeemed who make up the Church. The rest of the redeemed from the earth, those not part of the Church, must, therefore, have a different place prepared for them by God, perhaps as dwellers on the new earth, or in the new heaven (Revelation 21:1) - we are not told which.

The city is described as being 1400 miles (2200 kilometres) square, and shining with the brilliance and glory of God, who gives it light. It has twelve gates each made of a single pearl with one of the names of the twelve tribes of Israel on each gate. The walls of the city are made of jasper and have twelve foundations decorated with every precious stone. On the foundations are written the names of the twelve apostles of Christ (Revelation 21:9-21). It will be an amazing sight to see the river of life, clear as crystal, flowing from the throne of God and the Lamb down the middle of the great street.

"... On each side of the river stood the tree of life, bearing twelve crops of fruit, yielding its fruit every month. And the leaves of the tree are for the healing of the nations. No longer will there be any curse. The throne of God and of the Lamb will be in the city, and His servants will serve Him."

Revelation 22:2-3

The nations will walk in the light of the City and kings will bring their splendour into it. Those who have trusted Jesus Christ as their Saviour, in this life, will be there; they will look upon the face of God and reign with Him forever (Revelation 21:9-22:5).

When the Lord Jesus returns, He will come with rewards for His redeemed people, and judgement for those who have rejected Him. What we receive from Him, salvation or condemnation, is our own choice and will be our situation forever. It is an awesome and sobering exposé. What we are at the end of time is what we will be throughout all eternity: saved or lost forever and ever.

> *"Let him who does wrong continue to do wrong; let him who is vile continue to be vile; let him who does right continue to do right; and let him who is holy continue to be holy. Behold, I am coming soon! My reward is with Me, and I will give to everyone according to what he has done."*
>
> Revelation 22:11-12
> (See also Isaiah 40:10; 1 Corinthians 3:11-15 & 4:5;
> 2 Corinthians 5:10)

All the prophecies relating to the return of the Lord Jesus Christ are for all those who will take heed of them. We should all read and take them to heart, for the time is near; He is coming soon.

> *"Blessed is the one who reads the words of this prophecy, and blessed are those who hear it and take to heart what is written in it, because the time is near."*
>
> Revelation 1:1-3

> *"The angel said to me 'These words are trustworthy and true. The Lord, the God of the spirits of the prophets, sent His angel to show His servants the things that must soon take place.'*
> *"'Behold, I am coming soon! Blessed is he who keeps the words of the prophecy in this book.'"*
>
> Revelation 22:6-7

*   *   *   *

We have now reached the end of this brief introductory look at some of the prophecies in the Bible concerning the return of the Lord Jesus Christ. It is our hope that it has helped you, the reader, to understand what things lie ahead concerning God's prophetic plan. It is also our hope that by it you will be encouraged to seek further from the Bible, God's word, what He says about the amazing events that He tells us will surely happen before too long. They are written, not to scare or frighten, though initially they may well have that effect on us, but rather to warn us and to show that God really does purpose to bring an end to wickedness and evil in this world. They also show that He desires as many as will believe in His Son Jesus Christ, who died for our sins on the cross, to put their faith and trust in Him while they may.

It is also our great hope that all should know Jesus Christ as their own Saviour and Lord. For this reason, I have included the following chapter and trust that it will be of help.

13

And Finally . . . How Can I Be Saved ?

After reading all that has gone before, you may be concerned about where you stand before a holy, righteous and just God. Firstly, let us see what God says in His word about His thoughts and attitude towards mankind (in all quotations, emphasis has been added).

> "The Lord is not slow in keeping His promise, as some understand slowness. He is patient with you, **not wanting anyone to perish**, but everyone to **come to repentance**."
>
> 2 Peter 3:9

> "This is good, and pleases **God our Saviour, who wants all men to be saved and to come to a knowledge of the truth**. For there is one God and one mediator between God and men, the man **Christ Jesus, who gave himself as a ransom for all men** - the testimony given in its proper time."
>
> 1 Timothy 2:3-6

So what are we to do?

Well, God tells us in the Bible that we have all sinned (as if we needed to be reminded) and come short of what He expects of us (Romans 3:23). The problem is that He also tells us that there is nothing we can do to put right our sinfulness and shortfall ourselves.

*"No man can redeem [buy back] the life of another or give to God a ransom for him - the ransom for a life is costly, **no payment is ever enough** - that he should live on forever and not see decay."*

Psalm 49:7-9

But God loves us so much that He decided to come from heaven to earth as man to be our ransom, and to take upon Himself the punishment that our sins deserve.

Two thousand years ago, Jesus Christ came into this world to be our Saviour, by dying on a cruel Roman execution cross and taking God's judgement against our sins for us, so that we could be forgiven and go free.

*"He [Jesus] was pierced for **our** transgressions, He was crushed for **our** iniquities; the punishment that brought **us** peace was upon Him, and by His wounds **we** are healed. **We** all, like sheep, have gone astray, each one of **us** has turned to his own way; and the Lord has laid on Him [Jesus] the iniquity of **us** all."*

Isaiah 53:5-6

But it doesn't end there. Three days after Jesus died and His body was laid in a tomb, He rose from the dead. Jesus is alive!

*"Christ died for our sins according to the scriptures, ... He was buried, ... He was **raised on the third day** according to the scriptures."*

1 Corinthians 15:3-4

And because of this, all God requires us to do is to repent and simply believe and trust in Him as our Saviour, and He will freely forgive us our sins.

The Bible tells us:

*"For God so loved the world that He gave His only begotten Son, that whoever **believes** in Him should not perish but have eternal life."*

John 3:16

In another place, Jesus Himself said:

*"I tell you the truth, whoever hears My word and **believes** Him who sent Me has eternal life and will not be condemned; he has crossed over from death to life."*

John 5:24

God is still waiting today for people to repent of their sins, that is, to have a different attitude in their sinful heart and life: to change for the better. He longs for us to believe what He says about His way of salvation, and to trust His loving forgiveness. This is freely offered to everyone who believes in His Son, Jesus.

At the end of our short lives comes death. After death ... eternity. We need to ask ourselves, "Where will I spend eternity?" What will your answer be? Trust in Jesus Christ now for the forgiveness of sins and you will receive His free gift of eternal life. He will also give you His Holy Spirit to be with you forever and to guide and help you on your Christian pathway (John 14:15-17).

So:

"Believe on the Lord Jesus, and you will be saved."

Acts 16:31

You can ask God to help you right now by saying a simple prayer something like this:

"Lord, I know I'm a sinner and that my sins deserve your righteous judgement. Please help me to understand and believe that you love me; that Jesus died on the cross for my sins, and rose from the dead, so that I may receive your forgiveness and have eternal life. In Jesus' name, Amen." (Remember, saying this prayer doesn't save you; believing in your heart does!)

If you truly repent and believe, tell someone! You will only grow spiritually if you read God's word, the Bible. Also, it will be of great benefit to you if you meet with other Christians for mutual help, support and encouragement.

May God bless you.

Bibliography

The following list of book titles are those that I personally have found very helpful over the years. I have included them here for those who wish to study the subject further and are wondering which book or books to buy. Those that I consider particularly enlightening I have put "Recommended" at the end.

(**N.B.** It is not known whether all of these books are still available. If your local bookshop cannot obtain them, try the Web!)

Randall N. Baer, *Inside the New Age Nightmare* (Huntingdon House Publishers, 1989). (Recommended)

Charles H. Dyer, *The Rise of Babylon* (Tyndale House Publishers, 1991).

Alfred Thompson Eade, *The Second Coming of Christ* 'The New "Panorama" Bible Study course No. 3' (Fleming H. Revell Publishers, 1966). (Recommended)

Alfred Thompson Eade, *The Book of Revelation* 'The New "Panorama" Bible Study course No. 4' (Fleming H. Revell Publishers, 1970). (Recommended)

Sam Gordon, *Worthy is The Lamb* - *A walk through Revelation*

(Ambassador Publications, 2000).

Dave Hunt, *A Cup of Trembling* (Harvest House Publishers 1995). (Recommended)

Dave Hunt, *'How Close Are We?'* (Harvest House Publishers, 1993). (Recommended)

Thomas Ice & Timothy Demy, *Prophecy Watch* (Harvest House Publishers, 1998). (Recommended)

Dan Juster and Keith Intrater, *Israel, the Church and the Last Days* (Destiny Image Publishers, 1990/91).

Tim LaHaye and Thomas Ice, *Charting The End Times* (Harvest House Publishers, 2001). (Recommended)

Tim LaHaye, *Revelation Unveiled* (Zondervan, 1999).

Tim LaHaye, *Understanding The last Days* (Harvest House Publishers, 1998).

Rev. Clarence Larkin, *The Second Coming of Christ* (Published by the Rev. Clarence Larkin Estate, 1918).

Charles Ryrie, Joe Jordan and Tom Davies, *Countdown To Armageddon* (Harvest House Publishers, 1999).

About the Author

Richard Salmon, the youngest of three brothers, was born in the village of Havenstreet on the Isle of Wight, England, in 1951. He went to Sunday School at St. Peters Church of England, Havenstreet, and later served at the alter until the age of about thirteen. Even at a young age he believed that God existed and that Jesus was the Son of God who came to earth as man - that He died on the cross, rose from the dead and ascended back into heaven. The problem was, he never understood why!

He left school at the age of fourteen and started a boat building apprenticeship. But his thoughts were of distant lands and travelling the world.

After a brief spell in the Royal Marines and a short time back at boat building, at the age of seventeen he went to sea in the Merchant Navy. This was the start of a downward spiral into the depths of sin and, ultimately, his deep conviction that all was not well with his soul. As Richard says in his book:

"While I was a deck hand in my teens on a Merchant ship docked in St. John, Newfoundland, an elderly Christian man came aboard and gave me a New Testament. It was like handing me a time bomb! . . . the New Testament that he gave me was what the Spirit of God used to convict me that I was not right with God and that hell awaited the pleasure of my company."

133

It was not until two years later, in New Zealand, that Richard finally surrendered himself to Christ and received forgiveness of sins and eternal life. He was twenty years old.

Now, in his fifties and with well over thirty years of Christian experience behind him, Richard is happily married to his wife Jane. They live in Newport on the Isle of Wight, England, where they fellowship with other Christians at Bethany Evangelical Church. He occasionally preaches and ministers the word of God.

ISBN 1-41205484-2

9 781412 054843